RUDOLF STEINER (1861–1925) called his spiritual philosophy 'anthroposophy', meaning 'wisdom of the human being'. As a highly developed seer, he based his work on direct knowledge and perception of spiritual dimensions. He initiated a modern and universal 'science of spirit', accessible to anyone willing to exercise clear and unprejudiced thinking.

From his spiritual investigations Steiner provided suggestions for the renewal of many activities, including education (both general and special), agriculture, medicine, economics, architecture, science, philosophy, religion and the arts. Today there are thousands of schools, clinics, farms and other organizations involved in practical work based on his principles. His many published works feature his research into the spiritual nature of the human being, the evolution of the world and humanity, and methods of personal development. Steiner wrote some 30 books and delivered over 6000 lectures across Europe. In 1924 he founded the General Anthroposophical Society, which today has branches throughout the world.

BUTTERFLIES

Beings of Light

RUDOLF STEINER

Compiled and edited by Taja Gut

RUDOLF STEINER PRESS

Translated by Matthew Barton

Rudolf Steiner Press
Hillside House, The Square
Forest Row, RH18 5ES

www.rudolfsteinerpress.com

Published by Rudolf Steiner Press 2013

Originally published in German under the title *Lichtwesen Schmetterling: Drei Vorträge mit ergänzenden Ausführungen* by Rudolf Steiner Verlag, Dornach, in 2009. For further information see Sources, p. 80

A catalogue record for this book is available from the British Library

ISBN: 978 1 85584 375 2

Cover by Andrew Morgan Design
Typeset by DP Photosetting, Neath, West Glamorgan
Printed and bound by Gutenberg Press Limited, Malta

Contents

Introduction: The Butterfly Being

by Wilhelm Hoerner

The purest colours we see on earth are the colours of the rainbow, and the green and blue colours on butterfly wings. I call them the purest colours because they contain absolutely no coloured matter, arising instead through a special interplay of darkness and light. The iridescence on butterfly wings does not depend on pigment but is a phenomenon of refracted light. The 'archetype' of this phenomenon can be seen in the heavens. Behind the atmosphere of sun-imbued light and air the black background of the cosmos is brightened to the loveliest blue of the sky, without any material substance. And when, by contrast, light penetrates to us through dark layers of cloud, we experience the many shades of red and yellow at sunrise and sunset—again, in a pure and immaterial form. Thus these colours in the heavens arise through the 'deeds and sufferings of light' in Goethe's phrase. If we take this somewhat mysterious saying seriously it leads us into a domain of living being, a cosmos that is not merely dead matter but alive, sentient and intelligent in remarkable ways. Likewise those strange and wonderful beings the butterflies can help us rekindle a sense—lost to many people nowadays—of a world of spirit that is far more profound and resonant than we often suspect.

The fully developed butterfly is borne on wafting currents of air. It actually scarcely touches into moon-governed elements of earth and water, for it belongs inherently to the higher cosmos (see page 44). Its three preceding stages of development—egg, caterpillar and pupa—are bound to the earth. The emerging butterfly, however, is entirely given up to warmth, light, air and sun. Liberation from the earth element extends so far that seeking a mate, mating and laying eggs are possible without any further intake of food. In some species, the organs for eating are vestigial. The fact that butterflies visit flowers so eagerly and pollinate them is to do with their pleasure in the sweet dessert of nectar. As caterpillars, by contrast, they fed with such frenzy that often their skin had to burst to allow them to go on growing. However, butterflies gladly seek out water in moist woodland groves, for without it they would dry out too quickly in their brief butterfly life.

Now let us attend to each of the four great stages of metamorphosis in detail.

The egg

The eggs of butterfly species—we know of around 165,000—are already natural artworks of a diversity hard to comprehend. Certain egg shapes indicate particular species. They can be perfectly spherical or hemispherical, or shaped like rice-grains, or scales, or flat lentils. Others resemble loaves of bread or miniature bottles, and still others are cone-shaped, spindle-shaped or like cylindrical barrels. Eggs can stand upright or lie flat. Their size varies from 0.25 to 2.6 mm. They are glued fast to their base, usually the underside of leaves of the preferred fodder plant. Their surfaces are likewise very diverse, with between 20 and 50 flutes and ribs. As well as very smooth eggs there are coarse- and fine-grained surfaces, or ones textured with a woven network. We might wonder what purpose all this has—but we ask it in vain. These things simply are.

Each egg has tiny entrances called micropyles for the

sperm which fertilizes it the moment it is laid, and for penetration of the air and moisture which the embryo needs in order to develop. The way in which eggs are laid, and where they are laid, is also very varied: singly or in clusters of 40 to 60. For instance, the peacock butterfly can lay up to 150 eggs in 30 seconds in the upper part of a stinging nettle. The gypsy moth attaches its clutch of 2000 eggs to the branch of a tree and covers them with the brown hairs from its abdomen so that the whole thing looks like a sponge or fungus and, protected in this way, can survive the winter. Some species, such as the geranium argus, have to embark on a flying quest lasting several days to seek out the fodder plant for the next generation. The geranium argus lays its eggs on the base of the style of the rare *Geranium palustre*, and therefore the following conditions are necessary: the female butterfly must be fertilized, then it must find the fodder plant, often after a long search; and the plant's flower must be fully open to give access to the style. Once again we may wonder why things have to be so complicated. It gives us a sense, though, of infinite harmony, balance and integration throughout the natural world.

At caterpillar stage, the numerous types of brown argus live on grasses, which is why the female lets her eggs fall into clumps of grass as she flies over them. All forms of egg laying, however, ensure that sunlight can always reach, illumine and warm up the eggs or the whole area where they are deposited.

We will see in the course of this book how warmth, light and air embody a transition from the spiritual world of divine creation into the elemental precursors of what we nowadays call matter, and that butterflies, in their immaterial delicacy, offer us an image of this transition. We will see further how the butterfly's wings, with their scales and glaze, continually return spiritualized matter to the cosmos, the living world of spirit. We can trace this process in a twelvefold metamorphosis from egg through to flying butterfly.

The first stage of this path of transformation is the egg in the mother insect's body, ornately formed in all its diversity as described above. This egg, laid into a sun-illumined place, is fertilized at laying by the sperm deposited at mating in the female's sperm sacs. Here the egg experiences its first contact with the earth. After just a few days the egg's form can degenerate, and its colour darken. This is a sign that the germinal larva has triggered creative chaos within the egg substance and that embryonic development has begun. The tiny caterpillar forms at between 3 and 20 days, depending on the species and weather conditions. That is the second stage of metamorphosis—we can call them 'chaos' and 'formation'. The third stage is the hatching of the caterpillar. The tiny creature with black head and thin body has now consumed all the stores in the egg and gnaws a hole in the eggshell to emerge. These minute larvae, black in most species, immediately turn their attention to the egg case once they have hatched: as the first food of their new existence they eat it all up, down to the soil it may be stuck to. The eggshell is not made of chitin, the chief structural material of insects, but of a protein-fat compound. Egg form, embryo growth and hatching of the caterpillar are thus the first three stages of butterfly metamorphosis.

The caterpillar
The caterpillar likewise passes through three clearly marked, metamorphic stages. The tiny, newly-hatched creature is usually referred to as a worm. The worm in an apple is however of course not a worm like an earthworm, but the

caterpillar of the coddling moth. People have also long spoken of the 'silkworm' when in fact this is the caterpillar of the silkmoth. 'Caterpillar' is thought to relate to a Middle English word *piller*, meaning *pillager* or *plunderer*, though it also derives from a French word for 'hairy cat'. The scientific term is larva. The *Lares* were guardian deities, good spirits of the house, in ancient Roman times, whereas *larva* refers to an evil ghost, spectre or mask. Since the eighteenth century it has been used to identify a stage of insect development.

Here we discover a key principle in the life of butterflies—the radical difference of the four stages of egg, caterpillar, pupa and butterfly. When we look at a caterpillar it would be hard to know without being told that this might ever turn into a butterfly, or indeed how this can happen. In the western, Christian culture of the seventeenth century, Maria Sibylla Merian[1] independently rediscovered the metamorphosis from the one to the other.

Caterpillars are fully disguised or camouflaged at this stage, and wonderfully adapted to their surroundings. Their host plant provides them with food. The green caterpillar of the brimstone butterfly is perfectly camouflaged when it rests on the mid-vein of its buckthorn leaf. Brown caterpillars, likewise, cannot be seen even from close up when they attach themselves to the little twigs of their host plant. The caterpillar of the purple emperor is green like its food, the leaves of the sallow. It overwinters in the tree's forking twigs, becoming brown there like the tree itself. In spring, after its first meal, it changes colour again and becomes green. The multicoloured markings of most caterpillars make them far more beautiful than the butterflies they will later become. This is true particularly of the large family of deltoid moths. We still do not fully understand how some caterpillar colours such as green develop, but many pages could be written about their ability to camouflage themselves and imitate their surroundings.

The fourth stage of metamorphosis can be termed 'growth and skin-shedding'. An alternation between eating, resting and eating again gives rise to uninterrupted growth. In their mode of relating to plant food, however, there are again six different possibilities: tiger moths can eat all types of plant; the silver Y (gamma moth) can eat many types of plant; the swallowtail a few types from one plant family, while the mountain apollo can eat only one type of plant. Most caterpillars feed on the outside of plants, but the leafminers and borers feed inside the plant, in the thin layer between the upper and lower surface of a leaf.

The external skin of the greedily eating caterpillar cannot grow with it. The creature gradually feels as though it were being strangled. It can grow due to its capacity to, literally, burst its skin. This is not a very pleasant process. The caterpillar becomes restless and oversensitive, and stops eating, and instead—often after a lengthy journey—finds a place to shed its skin. Once it has found this, it will some-times sit there completely motionless for up to three days, fixed or woven to the spot. This growth pause can last more than a week in some species—the caterpillar cannot budge.

Discarding the old and now rigid external skin—com-posed of the insect-structuring substance chitin—is possible because the still living underlayer of skin lies along the length of the caterpillar's body as though in folds, awaiting its lib-eration. Now the old, rigid external skin tears above the creature's head and neck. At the same time, glands exude a secretion between the outer- and underskin to help cast the old one. The caterpillar stretches its head and the thorax segments, with their newly grown, six true insect legs, through the tear. Using these legs, it can now grasp hold of the solid surface beneath and pull its whole body out of the old, hard skin, which remains stuck behind it. Casting a skin like this is hard work since the coverings over mouth, respiratory openings and anus, belonging to the outer blastodermic layer, have to be changed as well. This is why the caterpillar remains weak and sensitive for a while after shedding a skin. Some species—such as the puss moth—consume the laboriously removed old skin like the eggshell. The caterpillar sheds its skin at least twice, and four or five times in most species. The clothes moth has to endure the travails of 13 to 17 skin-castings.

The extended, roller-shaped body of the caterpillar is so uniform in shape that its head, thorax and abdomen—which can be clearly seen in the butterfly—can scarcely be distinguished. Slight indentations divide the caterpillar's body into segments. To the head and the three chest rings, which bear the three pairs of true insect legs, are attached ten equal abdomen segments. Thus the creature has 14 limbs. Five of these abdominal limbs have another pair of legs each. These 'stomach feet' are actually skin extrusions (prolegs) without further subdivisions. Each foot has many circular bristle-hooks by means of which the caterpillar can attach itself firmly. The last pair of legs, on the penultimate segment, is called the anal proleg. When a caterpillar moves, the pairs of legs are sequentially advanced starting from the end of the body. This makes it seem as if a wave is streaming forwards through the caterpillar and bearing it onwards. Inchworms (geometer moths) have only five pairs of legs and, as they crawl, perform an upward loop with their whole body.

As to the multiplicity of colours, shapes and skin extrusions in caterpillars, we will restrict ourselves here to a word about their 'fur' or hair covering. Thaumetopoeinae moth caterpillars can have up to 360,000 stinging hairs growing on a single individual. Each hair is only 0.2 mm long and 0.003 mm thick, and so fragile that we still do not know whether their sting is mechanically caused or is due to the secretion of poison. This species bears the name of 'processionary' caterpillars because they live in communities and process one behind the other in long rows from their host tree to sleeping quarters and back. They have an extraordinary sensitivity to even the slightest movements of the host plant, and to the warmth, light, air and moisture in their surroundings. With six tiny eyes on each side of their head, some researchers believe that they cannot see anything clearly.

After the metamorphic stages of growing and casting skins, the other major aspect of the life of every caterpillar is its capacity to transform sunlight into silken threads. This however is preceded by the sunlight's transformation into green foliage and other earthly substances. Green vegetation—mainly from leaves but also other parts of plants—is absorbed by means of strong mandibles. Many types of caterpillar have a recess in their upper lip which acts as a kind of conduit to hold the edge of a leaf while gnawing it. Some eat 'everything on their plate'—or in other words consume the whole leaf down to its stump and stalk. Others merely chew round the edges or eat holes in the leaf. Still others leave the mid-vein and side-veins behind. Certain types of caterpillar can eat almost all of a plant, including seeds, roots or bark, and also wood, compost and very dry substances such as wax. They can even consume skins, hair or feathers. Only ferns and moss never seem to be on the menu. Given the unbounded rapaciousness of caterpillars, we might immediately think of them as 'pests'. In mixed woodland of leaf and needle trees, damage caused by mass reproduction always stays within limits. They only become harmful where unnatural monocultures are grown in woodland and agriculture—and thus human beings are the primary cause of increased damage. Around 200 creatures live on and from the oak, for example; the majority of them are insects, including 69 species of butterfly—though of course not all species live on one tree at the same time. This 'population' does not however cause oaks to die off. On the contrary, the life of such creatures keeps the trees' overburgeoning vitality in wholesome equilibrium with the rest of nature.

We should learn to see that this uninterrupted devouring of plant material, and the outer skin that cannot grow as the caterpillar does—thus giving rise to a repeated sense of the creature's inner suffocation—is actually a kind of ongoing self-sacrifice for the sake of future life. When it emerges from its egg the silkworm weighs 0.47 milligrams. By the end of its caterpillar development after 33 days it weighs 3.65 grams. To fully grasp the dimensions of this growth, we can draw the following somewhat outrageous comparison with human growth. Someone who weights 3.5 grams at birth would end up weighing 27.18 tons after 33 days if he grew at the same rate as the silkworm! This can give us an inkling of the kind of sacrifice involved. The caterpillar is completely unprotected in this process, and has no real means of defence. If two out of 100 butterfly eggs reach their goal of becoming butterflies, stocks of the species will survive. In an undisturbed biosystem, the remaining eggs, caterpillars and pupae serve as food for other creatures.

The many types of caterpillar gland are striking—skin glands for gland hairs, scent glands for the extruding osmaterium, stomach glands, wax glands, salivary glands, hormone and sex glands. The two characteristic and most important gland types in caterpillars are the spinning glands and skin-casting glands. Four different types of skin-shedding glands participate in skin-shedding and the metamorphosis into a pupa. The two spinning glands are so powerful that they account for a quarter of the caterpillar's body weight. Loop-shaped, they lie either side of the gut and can be five to six times longer than the whole creature. The raw material for the spinning glands is formed in the fatty tissue which absorbs the content of the gut. The spinning glands transform these provisions into fluid silk substance. The secretions of both spinning glands run together in the spinneret and emerge from there at the caterpillar's lower lip. Whatever caterpillars make from the silk is only possible by turning and rotating their head together with the upper body, also in a backwards direction. All caterpillars can spin silk, but the way they use it varies greatly: as guiding thread to find their way back into their lair, as protective nest material or as swaying camouflage. In order to crawl up a pane of glass, caterpillars glue a knitted ladder of threads to the surface and mount by that means.

The caterpillar of the white admiral will saw through an aspen leaf at its broadest place to cut off the pointed end. Then it spins together the two outermost parts of the remaining leaf, weaving back and forth with silken threads. As they emerge from the caterpillar, these threads are still moist, but as they dry they shorten so that the two edges of the leaf are pulled towards each other, eventually forming a closed leaf-bag, The caterpillar spends the winter in this small dwelling, surviving hoar frost and ground frost there. Left to itself the leaf would fall from the tree like other leaves.

But the caterpillar 'knows' this! This is why, before even starting to build its winter dwelling, it spins the base of the leaf so firmly to its twig that neither autumn winds nor winter frosts can remove the leaf and the delicate silken weft. In all such arrangements, a super-temporal intelligence is at work, simultaneously creative in past, present and future. We have grown accustomed to calling this 'instinct', meaning a natural drive to particular modes of behaviour. The great insect researcher Jean-Henri Fabre said that instinct is the work of a divine intelligence[2] and this cannot easily be disputed. We repeatedly see signs of cosmic intelligence at every stage of a butterfly's development. This is equally true of the astonishing capacity to overwinter, which shows only small variations: 3.5 per cent of all species overwinter as eggs, 66 per cent as caterpillars, 28 per cent as pupae and 1.5 per cent as butterflies. These latter include the peacock butterfly, the small tortoiseshell and the brimstone butterfly.

After this little detour relating to a special use of silk and overwintering capacities, let us pursue the silken thread a little further. This silk originally derives from the green foliage the caterpillar eats, which in turn is due to the sun's effect on the earth. The long, fine strands of silk—2000 metres of it weigh only 0.2 grams—give us a tangible image of the weaving light ether in interplay with the element of water.[3] As it spins its threads, therefore, the caterpillar is already accomplishing a kind of raising of the elements into the realm of lightness. Silk is a unique natural product. A silk thread can be stretched by up to 20 per cent, then contract again when released.

Five thousand years ago, the silk moth in China was the first domestic animal. Revered as divine, great care and attention were lavished on it. On a hill in the emperor's garden stood a temple to the silk goddess. There, surrounded by mulberry bushes, was a bright, white altar where the 'silk seeds'—the eggs of the silk moth—were ritually washed. At a great spring festival the empress gathered the mulberry leaves with a small golden sickle as food for the 'noble silk worms'. After their ceremonial dousing the eggs were then entrusted to the care of the six 'caterpillar mothers'. For millennia, on the same day each year the wives of the nobility carried out this nationwide rite in the Middle Kingdom for the 'ancestress of the silken thread'. As early as 2000 years before Christ there was a dedicated 'silk calendar' that made this possible. The least smells or noises were banished from the silk moth's 'birth chambers'. In early times, the caterpillars were fed 48 times each day with very finely chopped mulberry leaves. The caterpillars could only be cared for by young women aged between 16 and 25. They were required to avoid certain foods, to dispense with wearing any perfume, and must be neither sick nor sad. They moved or floated silently and with utter calm through the 'nurseries'. If anyone left a door open they were dismissed. Millennia of familiarity with the breeding and care of these most delicate creatures also refined and educated the people themselves, as a major contribution to the loftiness and delicacy of Chinese culture. The word 'culture' itself, of course, is closely related to 'cultivation' and has always been enhanced by care of and reverence for the natural world.

Transformation of sunlight into silk is the fifth stage of the butterfly's twelvefold metamorphosis. A caterpillar is a perfectly adapted and complete being for its particular stage of life and its environment. Each time a skin is shed a caterpillar reappears. At the end of this caterpillar existence, however, a radical metamorphosis occurs, in which the future plays in prophetically. What is still to develop announces itself as the delicate modelling on the pupa of eyes, feelers and wings of the future butterfly. Only from this future perspective—that is, as seen in terms of the whole cycle—is the caterpillar still an unfinished and therefore transitional being. The polarity of complete versus 'transitional', of present existence and future development, is also a human characteristic. This polarity is not just an outward fact or a true paradox, but we can see it rather as a manifestation of the uninterrupted interplay between the externally invisible world of spirit and the visible earthly world. It is part of being truly human that we not only endure this tension but also slowly learn, in it and through it, how we can grasp the meaning of our human existence on earth. The multiple transformations in butterfly development also conceal within them archetypes of the spiritual advancement of each individual human being and of all humanity.

When the time draws near for the pupa stage, the caterpillar stops feeding. It fasts completely and cleanses itself of all digestive remnants. Then, in many species, a restless wandering begins: long journeys are undertaken until the right place is found for the pupa to rest quietly. It has sometimes happened that caterpillars migrate in such large numbers across motorways to their pupating place that vehicle wheels go into a spin on the crushed mass of their bodies.

Rudolf Steiner spoke of four types of ether that correspond to the four elements, and embody a higher, finer, lighter and encompassing quality. These are:

Fire	Air	Water	Earth
Warmth ether	Light ether	Tone ether	Life ether

The butterflies likewise have four ways of accomplishing the difficult transition from caterpillar to butterfly. The hawk-moth and deltoid moth families have the hardest time. Their caterpillars delve to different depths in the earth and, at the end of a shaft, construct a kind of mortuary. Some also clad this chamber with splinters of wood they pull in and then cover these in silk to form a rich coffin. These structures, coagulated into a whole clump of earth, can sometimes be seen during ploughing or digging over a garden at spade depth. Some hawkmoth caterpillars dig themselves much deeper into the ground. There are African varieties that delve as deep as 7 metres so as to be close to moisture when conditions are very dry. The long shaft is lined with silk threads which the butterfly can use for crawling out when it emerges. If arid conditions persist, the pupating moth can 'lie in' for years and 'wait' until the host plant for the next generation has grown sufficiently. In its own life it has left behind the eating stage! It has become the expression of higher and lower spiritual beings and effects, and the harmonious accord between them.

The cabbage whites, swallowtails and other families behave quite differently. Their caterpillars seek a more or less vertical place on a twig, plant stalk, stone or the wall of a house and spin themselves a small cushion there of silk threads. The caterpillar holds fast to this in an upright position with its last pair of legs, the anal proleg. Then it bends its front part a long way backwards and attaches to the plant stalk or house wall a silk thread close to its middle body. With one rapid movement it then takes this thread backwards around its body and attaches it again on the other side, repeating these back-and-forth movements until its harness is strong enough. Now, like someone working high up on a mast or bridge it has a belt around its body. To superficial inspection, this kind of 'belt pupa' looks like a small twig just slightly raised from its base. The structural principle of all plants and trees, with their branches, twigs and leaves sticking out from them, is that of connection with the original plant yet at the same time striving or growing away from it in a new direction. The activity of the tone ether and of the element of water adhering to itself in the spherical drop are expressed in simultaneous separation and maintained connection. These two realms are active influences on the belt pupa in just as tangible form as are the life ether and element of earth upon earth pupae.

The third way of embracing caterpillar death is particular to the families of Nymphalidae or brush-footed butterflies, which include the peacock butterfly, the red admiral and the large and small tortoiseshell. They seek out a place that is as horizontal as possible on a twig, the eaves of a roof or the underside of a slab or coping with nothing beneath it. There they spin a firm cushion which they hold fast to with the anal prolegs, then let themselves fall backwards from it, ending up with their head downwards and swinging back and forth in every breeze. Their head and upper body are curved in a little, and grow fatter due to the accumulation of body fluid. This state is comparable to labour during human birth. After some hours the skin of the caterpillar's neck splits open and, with twitches and contortions, the caterpillar skin must now be stripped off in an upward direction. One can really say that the caterpillar 'does itself in'. Then comes the most difficult part of this kind of pupation: the caterpillar is, you remember, hanging by its back feet. But these are actually a kind of external skin that must be cast off as 'exuviae'. Once this skin has been pushed a long way upwards, the critical moment arrives, with the risk of falling off and thus voiding the whole process. The pupa-to-be now draws the end of its body out of the old skin but, as some researchers have discovered, jams it for a moment into the last rings of the abdomen to keep a hold. Very rapidly it pushes the end tip of the abdomen into the spun cushion. The end of the body of all pupae has a barb with fine hooks, the cremaster. Attached by this, the pupa hangs head down during its pupation. The old caterpillar skins, the disrobed exuviae hanging alongside, also have to be got rid of, and, if they do not fall off by themselves as the prolegs loosen, the pupa tries to do knock them off by twitching and turning.

Inside the pupa, tissue has already started to dissolve, and this fluid mass gives the still soft pupa skin a soft, extended drop form for a short while. But then, very quickly, a stretched sheath is modelled, with distinctive angles, ridges and jags, and hardens after about an hour. These freely hanging pupae, with head downwards, are passively exposed to the element of air with its dynamics, pressures and motions. The light ether that corresponds to this element here forms space inasmuch as it helps create boundaries for colours and forms. On the pupa's back and sides, points and zigzags ray outwards in relief. The form is more strongly and distinctively sculptured than any other type of pupa. Just as, in plants, the light ether exerts an out-drawing and space-encompassing influence in the extensions of growth towards the periphery, so here, on the metallic shimmering chrysalis that hangs freely in the air, it models gleaming golden, silver and copper coloured dots, spots and radiating lines.

The fourth way in which a caterpillar can die into the pupa is the best known. While still a caterpillar the silkworm spins its cocoon from a single very fine silk thread. The casing, which the caterpillar also attaches to something, is entirely closed off, and within it the transition from caterpillar to pupa occurs. There are many diverse kinds of cocoon made, pre-pupation, by caterpillars of the silk moth, tiger moth and snout moth families. The Bombycidae genus, which accounts for 1200 different species worldwide, includes the peacock moths, which in turn count among their family the biggest European moth with a wingspan of 13 cm, the Viennese emperor. There is no space here to give details of the manifold varieties of plant parts spun into these cocoons. The brown cocoons of some species often incorporate one or even two creel-type openings with sharp, outwardly directed points. These prevent an enemy entering from outside, without hindering the moth's emergence. Once the cocoon has been spun, the caterpillar lies down inside it for pupating with its head pointing towards the exit. Caterpillars that pupate in the earth also have to do this since the emergent butterfly cannot turn round to face the exit, whether in its hole below ground or in the silk cocoon. Both caterpillar and pupa vanish as it were from the outer world. Surrounded by the silk cocoon of spun sunlight, they die and live in their own micro-climate. External warmth cannot be held fast. The element of fire makes external form vanish from the perceived world. Warmth ether, by contrast, works into the sensory world in such a way that it kindles, incubates and ripens life. This process of maturation however can only occur within a new, firm sheath, in this case the chrysalis or pupa skin. This is sculpted from without to mirror the forms of head and thorax organs, while within is nothing but fluid. As only otherwise rarely in nature, the life ether forms a sheath from without here, in collaboration with the solidifying earth element. Together they 'embody' and consolidate the chrysalis. This is the sixth transformation. We have to realize however that the caterpillar as such has died away completely and dissolved, as will become clear in what follows.

The pupa

The larva or caterpillar is often highly camouflaged, and somewhat spectral and masklike. The word 'pupa' in Latin, meaning 'girl', indicates the future being who is as yet concealed—and of whom we may get a glimpse if we look into the 'pupil'. Most butterfly pupae form a conglomerate whole as single chrysalis with all appendages (feelers, feet, wing buds) closely bound to the body. This is called the 'pupa obtecta'. This was why Maria Sibylla Merian called such pupae 'date-stones'. This strange structure no longer absorbs food and scarcely moves. The pupae of small butterflies measure only 2 to 3 mm whereas those of the largest sphinx moths are 60 to 70 mm. The pupae of butterflies (as opposed to moths) often have yellow, green, greenish or dark dots and spots. Their metallic sheen earned them the name of 'chrysalis' (Greek, *chrysos* = gold) as long ago as Aristotle. Whereas the dragonfly emerges directly from the skin of the final larva stage without a pupa pause, all moths and butterflies undergo a 'complete transformation'. We should not overlook the fact that nature here takes a great leap. Once the caterpillar skin has been torn open, the initially bright green head part of the pupa emerges. As we saw, it is still very soft and almost unformed; and only gradually do the forms of subsequent organs impress themselves more clearly upon this soft skin, while within the previous caterpillar organs dissolve. Often very quickly, and within no more than 20 minutes, the external form is attained. If we compare the importance and size of the head part in caterpillar and pupa, we might be tempted to speak of an inversion whereby the body-accentuated form of the caterpillar is reversed in the pupa into an entity corresponding to the spiritual form of the butterfly. Invisible forces here work in from the periphery. The 'idea', the image of what is to develop, comes into focus as a prefiguring of the future. Caterpillar existence has ended and a completely new configuration, a rebirth into entirely new forms and with other modes of behaviour, is in preparation. Inside the hardened chrysalis, however, the reverse is happening. Tissues and organs are largely dissolved and melt into an unstructured, emulsion-like mass. This tissue dissolution (histolysis) is co-initiated by cells whose function can be compared with that of white blood corpuscles. If a pupa in this state is damaged, the body fluids run out leaving an empty casing. This seventh stage is the most sensitive in the butterfly's twelvefold metamorphosis.

Creation of the butterfly's future organs in the pupa is an extremely complex process in which the four elements and their corresponding four ether types collaborate harmoniously with the formative forces of each distinct species of butterfly or moth. Organ formation in the caterpillar occurs at a very early stage. Comparable to the embryo in the seed and the blastoderm in the egg, indentations form in the outer skin, often assuming a discoid shape and remaining in contact with the outer skin through a narrow channel. Just before pupation, these 'imaginal discs' are inverted over the surface of the skin through the connecting channel, similar to turning the fingers of a glove inside out. In other words, what originally intruded and was turned inwards like a gastrula is now completely reversed or extruded outwards. This inversion from within outwards is 'perhaps the most distinctive way to characterize a butterfly—as a reversal of the typical gesture of the animal which is involution (gastrulation)'.[4] This is particularly apparent in the wing scales which will be described below. The other organs too, such as feelers, compound eyes and legs, are present in a rudimentary form in the caterpillar and then fully formed in the pupa after inversion. The unstructured fluid mass at the first stage of the pupa is not entirely without movement. Within this protein-like fluid currents have been observed and also imaged. The dissolved substances of the former caterpillar body are conveyed to other places as a wholly new form seeks to arise. The tiny substance conglomerations of the imaginal discs are the sources of these growth processes, from which spring the formative forces of the newly forming organs, above all the wings.

Detailed descriptions of these spiritual-physical processes cannot be given here, but it is worth indicating two things. The element of air is twinned with light ether occurrences, which manifest in the former, and this element fills all the exterior space surrounding the pupa. The nine pairs of stigma and the breathing holes on both sides of the body allow air to reach the creature's interior, so that it is always in living communion with its surroundings. By this means, too, the necessary moisture is provided to the pupa and prevents it from drying out. The air's most characteristic attribute is its elasticity: it can be expanded and compressed. Pressure has an inner, maintaining effect and creates cohesion. In the pupa, everything is connected with everything and thus also with the external world, and this testifies to the influence of the air.

During tissue dissolution in the pupa, tiny crystals are preserved in the kidney tubules, the so-called 'Malpighian vessels'. In many species these are taken over into the forming body of the butterfly and usually excreted after emergence as 'pupal urine'. It seems too simplistic to regard this crystal formation, as is usually the case, as merely deposited and excreted products. In some species the crystals lie irregularly between and within the dense cocoon. In the case of the lackey moth the crystals are excreted around separate cocoon threads. The attachment web of belt and hanging pupae also contains crystals. These peculiarities have been discovered by magnifying 2500 times. The element of earth, as supporting and consolidating element, seems to be at work in these rigid crystal formations. Its corresponding ether, the life ether, shows its action in the membrane and chrysalis formation of the cocoon and pupa, which is also where the crystals appear. Here, then, we can conclude the eighth stage of metamorphosis, that of new configuration within the pupa.

The emergence of the butterfly is one of the most moving things we can encounter in nature. We can easily perceive the end of the pupation period and the approach of butterfly emergence in the belt and free-hanging pupae. The wings shimmer in full colour through the pupa case and the abdomen wings loosen so that the lighter areas can be seen between them. Having observed the caterpillar dying into pupa existence, our expectation of the emergence of a beautiful butterfly may initially meet with disappointment when we see the new creature. In the case of the peacock butterfly pupa the front, shield-type part of the pupa bursts, due to pressure from within, along a kind of seam, a 'perforation point', and the butterfly draws in air. It thus increases its volume and can continue to burst the case asunder. Then first of all the delicate feelers appear and acquaint themselves with the air. The front pair of legs follows and the creature uses these to get a purchase on the casing so that the second and third pair of legs can get free. At the same time the miniature wings, furled up as lobes, emerge. As yet these are entirely unable to function. The newborn being finally draws its abdomen out of the case as well and immediately tries to find some kind of support for its legs within close proximity, by means of which it can climb upwards. This is because the wings can only unfurl and dry out in a hanging position. In a glass jar without any purchase for climbing, the butterfly will inevitably die.

Once the butterfly or moth has crawled upwards and found a suitable place to unfold its wings, it pumps body fluid into the wing veins. It absorbs air and the wings unfold to their full length. But after 10 to 15 minutes it is still not able to fly. The wings have to remain folded together in their rest position, dry out fully and stiffen. For this purpose the body fluid is sucked back into the body and excreted via the rectum. This 'pupa urine', or haemolymph, can also be somewhat reddish, as it is in the black-veined white. In olden times, if many such butterflies emerged at the same time, people saw the pupa urine as a rain of blood and said that war was coming.

The emptied butterfly veins then fill with air, a process which can take up to several hours. The outer air brings with it a world of fragrances, received as messages by the slowly waving feelers. The proboscis is hesitantly extended and drawn in again. Gradually the great moment approaches when the creature's new existence is wholly grasped. A shiver passes through its whole being, the wings spread wide for the first time and clap together once more. This testing and vibrating is necessary to achieve the right body temperature, and this too can sometimes take several hours. But then at last the butterfly takes wing and flies off into a world bordering on unearthly freedom.

In ancient Greek the word *psyche* means breath and soul, but also butterfly. What they both have in common is something delicate, fragile and striving towards higher freedom. Around the time of Abraham, human soul life first emerged in a more autonomous form than had previously been possible within family, tribal and racial groups. For this reason, the words Nelly Sachs (1891–1970) wrote about Abraham are spiritually precise:[5]

> O you
> from whose intimating blood
> the butterfly word *soul* emerged,
> upfluttering pointer into new uncertainty.

The butterfly

The butterfly is entirely wing. Over and above its actual appearance, this fact points towards the living environment of light, air and warmth. The spiritual image of the creature that has passed through the metamorphic sequence from egg through caterpillar and pupa appears in fullest form in the developed butterfly. The 'imago' or fully developed butterfly images its spiritual being—as far as this is possible—in the visible, sensory realm, after gradually approaching its own living archetype through transformational stages. The word *butterfly* in English and *Schmetterling* in German both indicate a connection with dairy produce—butter in English and cream (Schmetten) in north-German dialect. The nectar in blossoms is likewise viscous and sweet. Thus the butterfly is the cream, butter and nectar licker but also, itself, as enhanced and ennobled as these rich foods. The Czech word *smetana* ('cream') has the same derivation.

Looking now at the three last and highest stages of butterfly existence we must turn first to the tenth, the wings themselves. The shapes of all butterfly wings are reminiscent of the leaves of plants. Both the separate front and back wings and the two wings of each side folded together reveal leaf shapes. Like a plant leaf, too, the wings have an upper and underside, and veins which stiffen and give form to these fragile, delicate structures, dividing them into different areas. Some of the veins branch while others run all the way through to the wing-tips. They vary so much between species that they can help us with identification. Just as the respiratory system and skin belong to the outer blastodermic layer, so the wings should also be seen as extrusions from this realm. Already at the end of the caterpillar phase, as we saw, the tiny, in-turned germinal discs of the wings are inverted towards the outer skin. This outward inversion is a process that we repeatedly encounter in butterfly development, from the caterpillar to the pupa, from the breathing system to the wings, from hair to scales and structure—and we will come back to this theme. Compared with their span at the moment of emergence, the wings occupy an area 20 to 30 times larger at their greatest unfurling.

The importance of warmth and light for the butterfly cannot be overestimated. Even in order to fly it needs a certain muscle temperature, varying between different species. Small geometer moths can manage with 16 to 17°C. Larger hawkmoths or sphinx moths can require up to or over 40°C. By vibrating their wings they build up the temperature they need to fly, although they can take flight in an emergency without this. Nowadays we know that most butterflies have to raise their body temperature to 30 or 40°C. Other species warm themselves up by sunbathing in the most effective wing positions. In order to fly, though, back and front wings have to be connected so as to form a continuous surface. Lower species have a recess lobe in the fore-wing in which the hind-wing is held fast for this purpose. All other families have firm cilia on the front edge of the hind-wing which are held by a kind of bristle fringe on the rear of the fore-wing. When they fly, the firm edge of the fore-wings pushes forward into the air while the rear and side parts of the wings allow the air to stream away in waves as the wings beat—rather like a flag attached to a flagpole that flutters in the breeze. In fact there is a kind of spiritualizing tendency in the butterfly's flight as we will see below. Apart from dragonflies and hoverflies, butterflies are the best flyers amongst the insects. The different species have very different flying modes however, so that one can identify them by their flight alone. The most unusual of these is the whirring or hovering flight of the hawkmoths in particular. In horizontal flight they can fly at up to 15 m per second or 54 km per hour. It has been found that the hummingbird's wing-tips move in a lemniscate around an imagined horizontal axis as it hovers. The butterflies, however, are the only known flying creatures with a vertical lemniscate wing plane in their hover flight. The hummingbird hawkmoth accomplishes up to 95 wing beats per second. It can be observed on a July evening hovering in front of phlox or balcony geraniums, where it visits up to 25 blossoms a minute. To be able to fly freely, every butterfly has, in addition to its four wings, two feelers with organs for orientation, balance and detection of the distant scents of flowers and partners. These feelers or antennae are multi-sectional, usually thread-shaped and often very long in daytime butterflies. In male moths they are comb-feathered like a fern. Butterflies or moths therefore need three pairs of flying organs to fly freely, and thus are six-winged, like 'metamorphosed images' of spirit beings.

To allow a full picture of the butterfly to arise in us we need to keep returning in different ways to the elements of warmth, light and air. We should also remember that six-sevenths of all Lepidoptera are night-flyers. Carrington Williams gives the ratio of night-flying moths to butterflies in the British Isles as 20,000 to 70.[6] In the light of day we perceive the things of the external world. The inner world and that of spiritual beings are, by contrast, not dependent on outer light. They can be experienced, seen and acknowledged without it. In the mystery centres of olden times, people spoke of 'seeing the sun at midnight'. During their spiritual quests, the Druids withdrew into dark stone chambers (cromlechs) and shut out the sun's daylight, so as to perceive non-physical solar influences. Here it becomes apparent that the night, as well as the day, bears secret revelations. In his 'Hymns to the Night', Novalis says: 'The eyes which the night opens within us seem to us more heavenly than those shimmering stars.'

In the two final stages of metamorphosis we will consider the more tangible, visible aspect of butterflies' spiritualization of earthly substance, as Rudolf Steiner describes this from his spiritual research.

The scales

The upper and underside of the wings, the butterfly's whole body and parts of the legs are covered in scales or hairs. The scales are regarded as reconfigured hairs derived from skin cells. Thus they are, once again, an extrusion, here repeated many thousands of times. The wings of a butterfly can be covered in a million scales measuring 0.1 mm in length and 0.05 mm in breadth. The covering is often so dense that 200 to 600 scales can lie on one square millimetre. The scales are arranged like roof-tiles and their shape shows how the whole wing strongly resembles plant leaves—in butterflies the leaves of a wych elm, in moths the leaves of grasses. Like the wing itself, each scale also has an upper- and underside. The interstice is divided into chambers, is void of plasma and usually partly or entirely filled with air or pigments. Pigments are the deposits of waste and end products of metabolism. The human skin, too, acquires its coloration, especially sun tan, from the depositing of substances that have reached an end stage, have been combusted. In the butterfly's scales, black and light-sensitive pigments predominate, and give rise to luminous red, orange, yellow and shades of white. These are the same light-sensitive pigments that lend autumn woods their colourful appearance.

The blue and green colours, as well as various shades of black, arise in a quite different way, as will be described below. Like caterpillars, the butterflies are integrated into their surroundings in innumerably diverse and harmonious ways.[7] Here we can see how the upper- and underside of each species' wings is immersed in the light and shadow effects and colour qualities of its surroundings. We can only point to such symbiosis in passing.

Glaze

A further differentiation and last material refinement that goes beyond the eleventh metamorphosis of the scales is apparent in the 'glaze', a fine structure on one part of the wing-scales. Pigment colours on the active side of the colour scale, from white through yellow, red, brown and black, are metabolism end substances. The green, blue, violet and some black tones are based on something quite different, which can only be made visible through strong magnification. Under the microscope the surface of these scales does not appear smooth but instead is sculptured and modelled in the most manifold ways. It is not easy to describe these fine, sculptural forms in words. One has to reach for metaphors that are, however, hard to comprehend due to the structures' microscopic size—less than a thousandth of a millimetre. These forms, consisting of the finest chitin, can be inscribed on the scales in close-set rows like nurseries of miniscule fir trees. Others lie upon the scales in several layers of thinnest membrane, separated from each other by struts. One is reminded here of core iron in concrete structures. Meshwork and matting, sheets and platforms have been pushed up from the surface of the scales in a last, radical process of inversion and extrusion. The scale itself contains dark pigments while the pigment-free sculptured forms give rise to a delicate cloudiness obliquely illuminated by light. Just as the darkness of space appears a heavenly blue to us through the illumined veils of the atmosphere, and as dark, faraway mountains grow blue in the distance, so the same factors at work on the wings of a butterfly create a luminous blue sheen. Some of the structures are such that the blue remains constant however the light falls—as is the case with most of the blue butterflies. These structural colours can be exposed to sunlight for any amount of time without fading, and are thus lightfast. In contrast, the pigment colours vary in their light sensitivity. Both types of colour however mark the end of a twelve-stage sequence of development: pigment as the end product of chemical processes drawing on the element of fire; and formative forces at work in endless refinement via the tone ether and its dividing and structuring action, through to the 'dust' on the butterfly's wings. Rudolf Steiner speaks of the 'spiritualized matter of the butterfly wing'. In doing so he also invokes the goal of humanity's whole evolution on earth. Gradual spiritualization in a twelvefold sequence of metamorphosis is embodied for us in the butterfly.

EGG
1. Forming   2. Developing   3. Hatching

CATERPILLAR
4. Growing   5. Transforming   6. Pupating

PUPA
7. Dissolving   8. Configuring   9. Emerging

BUTTERFLY
10. Unfolding   11. Undergoing   12. Illumining
                            combustion

The 'manifold secret' (Goethe) of butterfly metamorphosis is a living image of the whole evolutionary path of spiritualization of the earth and human being, made visible before us. Birth, life and death acquire their intrinsic meaning through development and transformation over great spans of time, from the earliest planetary conditions through to far-distant ones in the future.[8] This process of transformation is also grounded in the fact that spirit and matter form a unity whose fruitful interaction can be recognized and furthered by the free spiritual activity of human beings.

In his lecture of 27 October 1923, Rudolf Steiner compares the emanation of spiritualized matter with a 'butterfly girdle encompassing the earth' that can be perceived by spiritual beings. On the following day he expands this picture to speak of a 'butterfly corona'. In astronomy, the name corona is given to the bright crown of rays that stretch out beyond the sun's disc and can be seen at a total eclipse of the sun. Thus spiritual beings and souls preparing for incarnation on earth see the earth surrounded by the crown of rays of spiritualized matter. This image of transformative potential gives them courage for their 'earthly sojourn'. Likewise the butterfly wings created by inversion, the scales and the glaze from within and without, are a natural phenomenon that point to a spiritual process. Our inner life after death is inverted, according to Steiner, into a whole outer environment around us, while the outer earthly environment, by contrast, inverts into inner experience.

Rudolf Steiner often spoke of the butterfly as an image of the soul's immortality: 'And the butterfly that emerges from the pupa would not exist if there were not an immortal soul' (11 August 1919). 'This is not merely metaphor [...] but a reality that forms part of the divine world order' (21 August 1919). This reality arises from the fact that both developed together in mutual correspondence and that in both a process of evolution is possible only through a series of metamorphoses. In the visible transformations of the butterfly we can experience a revelation of the spirit. By allowing the idea to light up in us that our consciousness is capable of transformation, and by nurturing this idea, we come to live in the spirit and in truth.

1. Woven Sunlight

From a lecture in Dornach, 19 October 1923

Let us consider for a moment the metamorphosis undergone by the creature that later turns into a butterfly.

As you know, the butterfly lays its egg, and from that egg a caterpillar emerges. The egg completely encloses and contains everything that later gives rise to the butterfly. The caterpillar emerges from the egg into the light-irradiated air. That is the environment into which the caterpillar emerges. The important thing to note is that the caterpillar really lives in the sunlit air.

This is something you can study when you're lying in bed at night and have lit your lamp, and a moth flies towards it and finds its death in the light. The effect of the light on the moth is such that it seeks its death. There you see how light acts on a living creature. [...] The moth casts itself into the flame at one moment, giving the whole of its moth substance over to the light; the caterpillar gradually weaves its caterpillar substance into the light, pauses at night, weaves by day and spins and weaves a whole cocoon around itself. The cocoon, the threads of the cocoon, are what the caterpillar weaves out of its own substance as it spins on in the flood of sunlight. And so the caterpillar, once it has become a chrysalis, has woven around itself, out of its own substance, the sunbeams to which it has merely given physical substance. The caterpillar, sacrificing itself, casts itself into the sunlight and weaves around itself the threads of the sunbeams, following the direction in which they go at any given moment. If you look at a silkworm cocoon you are looking at woven sunlight, but sunlight given physical form from the substance of the silk-spinning caterpillar itself. The result is an enclosed space so that external sunlight has in a sense been overcome within. You'll remember that when I described the Druid mysteries I spoke of the sunlight which enters the cromlech becoming inward.[9] The sun, which previously exerted its physical power, causing the caterpillar to spin its own cocoon, now exerts power on what is inward and interior, and out of this creates the butterfly, which then emerges. Then the whole cycle begins again [...]

If I consider what I bear within me as memories, this is a complex process. Below in the physical body a kind of egg formation occurs, though in a spiritual way. What happens within me when I perceive something which triggers a thought in me, which is pushed downwards, is like a butterfly laying an egg. In the etheric body[10] this bears a resemblance to the physical formation of the caterpillar, and in the astral body[11] it has an inner resemblance to the pupa, the cocoon. The transformation that occurs is similar to what happens to the caterpillar: the life of the etheric body sacrifices itself to the astral light, as it were weaves an inner, astral cocoon around the thought, and then memories emerge. While our momentary thoughts are represented in the plumage of birds, the wings of butterflies, shimmering with colours, are a spiritual counterpart to our memories. Thus we look out into nature and feel it to be enormously related and connected with us. [...]

2. Metamorphoses

From a lecture in Dornach, 8 October 1923

[...] When autumn approaches, and the butterfly is fully mature, it lays an egg, from which of course another butterfly does not immediately emerge. Instead of a butterfly—let's say a swallowtail—what people commonly call a 'worm' emerges—a caterpillar. So here we have this caterpillar: here is its head, on its back it carries spines; and it crawls lazily, slowly about—is really rather idle. Inwardly though it is not idle at all but spins threads out of its body, from which it forms a sheath or case around itself. So here is the caterpillar, and here the threads it spins out of itself to form a hard case. In the pupa the caterpillar gradually vanishes entirely, dissolves within these threads. Thus it encases itself in a cocoon that it attaches somewhere to a tree trunk. It first glues on the thread and then vanishes inside the casing. Here we have, therefore, the egg, the caterpillar and now what is called the pupa. The pupa hangs there for some time, then the creature within makes a hole in it and the butterfly emerges. Before a butterfly can do so, therefore, four things are necessary: first the egg, second the caterpillar, third the pupa and fourthly the butterfly itself. The egg is laid somewhere. The caterpillar crawls around. The pupa hangs firm and still, and the butterfly flutters about happily in the breeze and can in turn lay an egg again so that the whole cycle repeats.

People study this and observe it through a microscope. But the whole business is not as simple as their explanations might suggest. We have to study where the egg can live and how it lives, how the caterpillar lives, how the pupa lives and how, finally, the butterfly lives. If the egg is to hatch a caterpillar it sometimes needs only very little indeed, but it does need moisture in which some salt is dissolved. No egg can thrive without having some moisture with salt dissolved in it. Therefore the butterfly has to have the instinct for laying its egg where it can receive moisture containing salt. This is also true for bees and other such creatures. Bees also need the place where they lay their eggs to be permeated with salt—albeit a tiny amount. Few people consider this. It is enough if fog passes by, for this always has some saline moisture. [. . .] The moment the caterpillar emerges from the dark enclosed world of the egg, it emerges into the light and is continually in light. The caterpillar has sensory organs and comes out into the light. It is now a quite different entity from the egg. The egg has become transformed entirely into the caterpillar. And the fact that the caterpillar is exposed to light and has sense organs has an inner effect upon it. In certain other phenomena we see something similar but in more extreme form. I'm sure you have all witnessed what happens when you light a lamp or a candle and all sorts of insects are attracted to it and start fluttering about in the room, even hurtling into it and burning up. What causes this? Of course our caterpillar does not do it, but it also feels drawn to light in a similar way. Sunlight attracts the caterpillar in what I would call a voluptuous way, just as a candle flame can draw insects that hurl themselves into it. The caterpillar, though, cannot get up to the sun. If it were able to lift itself from the ground and fly upwards to the sun, we would soon have no cater-pillars left—they would all fly off. That's what they really want to do, but the earth's gravity holds them down. But a caterpillar really has the will or desire to merge with the light. It cannot do this, so what does it do?

Picture a ray of light. The crawling caterpillar now starts to spin a thread that entirely accords with the ray of light, is oriented to it. When rays of light are not there, at night, it rolls up the thread and then, when day comes, spins the thread again within the ray of light, reeling it in again at night and so on. And thus its pupa case is formed around it. There the caterpillar dissolves entirely into light, dies into light like the insect that is drawn to the flame. Instead of merging with the sun itself, the rays of light themselves, it spins its own body into these threads and makes what one calls a cocoon around itself. The silkworm caterpillar spins silk that contains light. If you take silk from a silkworm, therefore, you have really taken spun light. Earthly matter has here been spun towards light rays. And if you look at a pupa you're actually looking at nothing but spun sunlight, earthly substance that has been spun into sun rays.

So here's the pupa, and around it spun light. The fact that this is spun light means, of course that now something different happens from when an insect hurtles into a flame and burns up. If such an insect were able instead, as quickly as it hurls itself into the flame, to spin around itself a cocoon that was oriented to the flame's rays, the fire's power would give rise to a new creature within this cocoon. But the creature burns up and thus this cannot happen. It is interesting that this tells us what the insect fluttering around in the room at night and falling into the flame really desires. It wishes to reproduce, to perish so that it returns in a new form. But it is mistaken since it is unable to make a protective membrane for itself quickly enough. The caterpillar however has time to spin its membrane, and now the power of the sun, which is caught, imprisoned within the pupa, can create the butterfly within it. It then emerges as a sun creature, and can fly about as a sun creature.

You see, the insect that hurls itself into the flame does not really wish to die but desires to return in a different form. It wishes to be reconfigured by the flame. And so death is everywhere. Death is not what destroys creatures but, when it is properly conducted, only transforms them. That's the first thing. Secondly, there is a profound connection between everything in external nature. The butterfly is formed from light, but first the light has to be made into thread by taking up earthly matter to form a cocoon. All animal creatures are created out of light, as the human being also is through processes that occur by fertilization of the female egg which are protected by a membrane inside the human being. In truth it is light that creates a new human being in the mother's body, makes it possible for a human being to develop from and through light. We can see therefore that the butterfly arises from light that is first captured and internalized.

Now the butterfly flutters around in its many colours. Such colours exist in conditions that are greatly influenced by light. In hot tropical regions all birds are brilliantly coloured because the sun has greater strength there. So we can ask what is accomplished by the creative power in the sunlight, in imprisoned light. It produces colours, always brings forth colours. The same is true of the butterfly: it acquires its colours through the action of imprisoned light. We can only understand the butterfly as being created out of the entirety of light, which endows it with many colours.

The sun cannot accomplish this alone however. Let's go back to the egg, which is embedded in moisture, and in salt. Salt is earth, moisture is water. So we can say the egg needs earth and water to thrive. The caterpillar's whole being cannot just thrive in earth and water, thus for instance in dissolved calcium and water, but it needs besides moisture or water also air: both air and moisture. This moisture and air, which the caterpillar needs, is not just what the egg needs physically, but within this moisture lives what is called ether, and which, in the human being, I have described to you as the etheric body. The caterpillar acquires an etheric body and breathes by means of it. Through the etheric body it absorbs what is already spiritually present in the air. The egg is still completely physical, while the caterpillar already lives in the physical-etheric. But for the caterpillar it is hard to live in the physical-etheric. The caterpillar has far too much heavy earth substance in it. When the caterpillar comes into the light this is apparent in the fact that it starts spinning light rays out of itself in the form of its cocoon silk. The caterpillar would like to approach the light but cannot do so, for it has too much gravity in it. It cannot cope with what it is exposed to, and therefore it wishes to resolve into light, pour itself into light so as to go on living in light. So what does it do? It encloses itself from the earth with sun rays, making a cocoon around itself. The caterpillar closes itself off entirely in the pupa from physical earth forces. And now the pupa bears astral forces in the inner space where the 'worm' has dissolved—not earth forces any longer or etheric forces, but astral ones, entirely spiritual forces. These astral forces live in the imprisoned light. The imprisoned light always bears spiritual forces, astral forces within it, and these create the butterfly. And because the butterfly consists entirely of astral forces it can flutter about in the air, as the caterpillar cannot. It follows light and is no longer subject to gravity. By dedicating itself to light, the butterfly has removed itself from weight. We can also put it like this: it has matured into the I. In a way we see the butterfly fluttering around within an I. We human beings have our I within us, while the butterfly has it outside itself. The I is really light. This colours it.

We all say 'I' of ourselves, but what does this actually mean? Every time you say 'I' to yourself, a tiny flame shines in your brain, though this cannot be seen by ordinary sight. That is light. When I say 'I' to myself, I invoke light in myself. This same light that dyes the butterfly's wings is what I invoke in myself when I say 'I'. It is really extraordinarily interesting to observe that when one says 'I' this would be light in external nature if I were able to radiate it out into the world around me. I have imprisoned this I in my body. If I were able to emit it, I could create butterflies with it. The human I has the power to create butterflies, insects and so on. People today imagine things are so self-evident and straightforward. But in older times, when these things were still understood, their words contained such truths. In ancient Judaic culture the word 'Yahveh' meant the same as 'I', and only priests were allowed to speak it. Only priests had undergone the right preparation to know what this meant. At the moment a priest spoke the word 'Yahveh' he saw images everywhere of fluttering butterflies; and he knew that if he spoke it in such a way that he saw nothing, he had not spoken it with the right inner warmth of heart. When he saw butterflies everywhere, he knew he had spoken the word with the right inner warmth of heart. He could not have taught this to others without more ado without them going mad in consequence; and this is why priests first had to undergo long preparation. But what I say is true.

[...] You say 'I' and really you wish to create butterflies everywhere, since the I is light. But you cannot actually do so.

Instead, you feel a kind of resistance. And these are your thoughts. They arise because we cannot actually create butterflies with the light. The I thinks thoughts, which are really only images of the world of butterflies.

3. Born out of Light

From a lecture in Stuttgart, 15 October 1923

A butterfly lays an egg, and a caterpillar crawls out of it; the caterpillar spins itself a cocoon for pupation, and from the pupa the butterfly emerges. These things are studied and described—but without any awareness of the wondrous mystery underlying them. The butterfly lays an egg. This egg, firstly, has to be laid at the right time of year, and must become receptive to the whole context of the earth's solid or solid-fluid substance. Dissolved mineral substance, salt, is the thing most necessary for the egg to develop. And then comes the point where, apart from the element of earth, that of water—and with it the etheric—takes precedence. Fluid permeated by the etheric forms the caterpillar that hatches out of the egg. In relation to the egg we think primarily of the physical earth element. When we see the form of the caterpillar hatching out of the egg, what crawls out of the egg as the caterpillar proper is an ether-permeated, fluid, watery creature. Now the caterpillar has to develop through the influence of air. For the caterpillar, the most important thing is for it to come into connection with light; it lives really in light-pervaded air, but at the same time also experiences an inner relationship with astral qualities and, through this relationship to the astral, it absorbs light. This is the most important thing about the caterpillar—that it is exposed through its sensory system to the rays of the sun, the shining sun's light. [...] The caterpillar enters fully into radiant light, giving itself up to it, spinning physical matter from its body into or towards the rays of the sun. The caterpillar sacrifices itself into the sun rays: it wishes to merge with it, to be destroyed, but all destruction is birth. [...] The threads spun by the caterpillar each day are materialized, spun light.

Having spun these threads into a pupa, the caterpillar dissolves within it. Light itself is the cause of the spinning of the pupa. The caterpillar cannot hurl itself into the light but it gives itself up to it, creating a chamber in which light is enclosed. From above downwards the pupa membrane is created according to primal wisdom's laws of form. And the butterfly arises and forms after the caterpillar has prepared its enclosed chamber for the light. So here you have the whole process from the butterfly egg through to the shimmering colours of the butterfly—which is born out of light as all colours are born from light.

[...] We cannot actually penetrate this whole process except by picturing it artistically. The process that arises when the butterfly forms in the cocoon and emerges is born from light, and cannot be pictured in any other than an artistic way. A wondrous artistic element is what we engage with when we picture the process as it really is, quite factually. Just see the kind of awareness you develop when you know something in this way. It is a quite different mode of knowing from the modern, superficial kind of knowledge, which is really a way of not knowing. Everything becomes interesting when, with our whole embodied soul, we grow into the artistic creativity of the cosmos.

4. The Butterfly as an Image of the Immortal Soul

From a lecture in Dornach, 11 August 1919

Here we approach something that is so hard for people today to understand since our sensibility is scarcely prepared to engage with it. Nevertheless, it must be understood if there is to be any real talk of renewing society. We need to grasp the fact that social co-existence in future will depend on something that enables people to mutually support each other. This is something they need to take seriously in their exchange of ideas and feelings. If people wish to become social beings, the views they entertain together are not a matter of indifference. In future it will be necessary, in education, to move beyond the dominance of mere concepts that originate in science or industry. Concepts are needed that offer a foundation for the capacity of imagination. However improbable this may seem nowadays, efforts at socialization will get nowhere without, at the same time, offering people imaginative concepts—in other words, concepts that configure human sensibility in a quite different way from merely abstract concepts such as cause and effect, matter and energy and so on, derived from materialistic science. Such scientific concepts, all-pervasive today even in the realm of art, are useless for preparing the future life of society. In future, in our social dynamics, we must develop the capacity to understand the world in pictures once again.

I have repeatedly highlighted the importance of this, also in connection with education. For instance, as I have shown, if we connect closely with children we can easily convey the idea, say, of the immortality of the soul to them by showing them a butterfly pupa and showing them how the pupa breaks open and the butterfly emerges from it. After this we can tell them the following. Your body is like the pupa, and inside it lives something like a butterfly—except that it is invisible. When you die, this butterfly likewise emerges from you and takes wing into the world of spirit.

One works metaphorically—in images—with such comparisons. However, it is not enough merely to work out such metaphors intellectually, an approach which would remain under the sway of the scientific outlook.

The secret lies in this: that a child will only feel a picture really speaks to him if the adult truly believes in it. A real spirit of esoteric investigation will return us to a point where we no longer see in nature the spectral miasma which science gives us but will start to see imaginative qualities, true pictures. The butterfly emerging from the pupa really is an image of the soul's immortality, which the divine world order has transposed into the natural order. The butterfly would not exist, could not crawl out of the pupa, if no immortal soul existed. An image cannot exist in fact—and this is an image—if it is not based on truth. And all of nature is like this. What science gives us is phantom-like. We can only approach nature by knowing that it gives us true images of another realm.

5. Butterfly Beings and Plant Nature

From a lecture given in Dornach on 26 October 1923

[...] If, with a gaze schooled in initiation science, we survey the whole course of earth's evolution and everything that evolved with it from earlier planetary conditions,[12] we can turn firstly to the rich diversity of the world of insects. Just by using our feelings we can immediately sense that this shimmering, fluttering insect world relates in a special way to ancient evolution connected with Saturn and Sun stages,[13] with upper, airy conditions as opposed to lower watery conditions connected with Moon and Earth stages of evolution. Look at a butterfly: it flutters in shimmering colours in air filled and illumined with light. It is borne on currents of air. It scarcely touches watery conditions relating to Moon and Earth. Its natural element is the upper world. If we trace the development of this insect, remarkably it leads us back into very early stages of earth's metamorphoses. The butterfly wings that shimmer today in the light-illumined air first formed as disposition during the Old Saturn period and evolved further during Old Sun. There developed at that time what still enables the butterfly to be a creature of light and air. The sun has its own innate capacity to radiate light. But it owes its capacity to invoke shimmering, fiery qualities in substances to the influences of Saturn, Jupiter and Mars. And actually we cannot fully understand butterfly nature at all if we only seek it on earth. The forces active in butterfly nature have to be sought in the upper world, in Sun, Mars, Jupiter and Saturn. If we examine the wonderful process of butterfly development in more detail—on a previous occasion I described it in relation to human beings as the cosmic embodiment of memory[14]—we find if we look more closely that the butterfly flutters above and over the earth, borne on the air and shimmering with light. It lays its egg. Yes, anyone with a purely materialistic view will say that a butterfly just 'lays its egg'—since things of primary importance are entirely ignored by what passes for science nowadays. The real question in fact is this: what does the butterfly really entrust its egg to when it lays it?

Take a careful look at where butterfly eggs are laid and you will find they are always deposited where the sun's influence can reach them. The sun's influence does not just reach where the sun shines directly on the earth. I have often pointed out that farmers place their potatoes in the earth over winter, covering them in earth. This is because what comes from without during the summer as the sun's warmth and light is inside the earth during the winter. Potatoes freeze on the surface of the earth but do not do so if you dig a trench and place them in it, then cover them with earth. They remain good and wholesome there because the sun's influence resides within the earth over the winter. Throughout the winter we have to look for the sun's action and influence below ground. If for instance we dig down to a certain depth in December, we find the sun's July influence. In July the sun streams out its light and warmth upon the earth's surface and these gradually penetrate deeper. If, in December, we wish to seek the sun forces we had on the earth's surface in July, we have to delve into the earth, dig a trench, and then we find it at a certain depth. So there the potato is embedded in July sun. In other words, the sun is not just where people seek it with merely materialistic understanding but is present in many other places, in a way strictly regulated, however, by the seasons and by the influences of the cosmos.

The butterfly always lays its eggs where they can remain in some connection with the sun. So it is very inaccurate to say that the butterfly lays its egg in the earthly realm. It certainly does not. It lays its egg in the solar realm. The butterfly actually never descends as far as the earth. The butterfly lays its eggs wherever sun is to be found in the earthly realm, so that they can remain under the sun's influence. The eggs never in fact fall under the earth's sway.

Then, as you know, the caterpillar crawls out of the butterfly egg. The caterpillar hatches out and remains under the sun's influence but now also comes under another influence too. The caterpillar would be unable to crawl if another influence didn't come into play as well—the influence of Mars.

If you picture the earth [drawing] and Mars orbiting it, Mars currents are and remain everywhere above. It is less a question of Mars being in a particular position but that the whole Mars sphere exists; and as the caterpillar crawls about, the Mars sphere works upon it. Then the caterpillar enters the pupa stage and forms a cocoon. I have described before how this represents the caterpillar's devotion to the sun, how the thread it spins is oriented to the light. The caterpillar is exposed to the light, traces the raying lines of light as it spins, then pauses when daylight fades and then carries on spinning again. All this is really cosmic sunlight, sunlight permeated by matter. If you look at the silkworm cocoon for instance, used to make garments of silk, this contains sunlight spun into silkworm threads. Out of its own body the silkworm caterpillar spins its substance, oriented to the direction of sun rays, thus forming a cocoon around itself. But for this to happen it needs the influence of Jupiter. The sun rays have to be modified by the action of Jupiter.

Then, as you know, from the cocoon, from the pupa state, the light-borne, light-shimmering butterfly emerges. It leaves the dark chamber into which light could only penetrate as it does into the cromlechs of the ancient Druids, as I described to you before. Here the sun falls under the influence of Saturn, and only in collaboration with Saturn can the sun send light into the air in such a way that the butterfly can shimmer in the air in all its many colours.

And so, when we look upon a wonderful sea of flying butterflies, we have before us in the atmosphere something that really cannot be thought of as an earthly form but is, rather, borne to earth from above. The butterfly with its egg does not descend further than the sun's influence upon the earth. The cosmos gives the earth the gift of this sea of butterflies. Saturn gives the butterfly colours. The sun gives the power of flight, invoked by the sustaining power of light, and so forth.

Thus we can see it like this: butterflies are small beings strewed down upon the earth by all that exists as our sun and planetary system. The butterflies, and all insects in general, dragonflies and the other insects, are really gifts from Saturn, Jupiter, Mars and the sun. The earth could not actually produce a single insect, not even a flea, if the outer planets, together with the sun, did not give this gift of insect life. The fact that Saturn, Jupiter and the others can be so generous in their gifts as to let the insect world flutter down to us is due to the first two stages of evolutionary metamorphosis of our earth.

But now let us see how the last two metamorphoses, the stages of Moon and the present planetary condition of Earth, have played their part in all this. Even though, as we have seen, the butterfly egg is not entrusted to the earthly realm, we have to point out that at the beginning of the third metamorphosis, the Moon stage, butterflies were not yet as they are today. The earth was also not so dependent on the sun. At the beginning of this third stage of metamorphosis the sun and earth were still united, and only afterwards separated. For this reason, the butterflies were not yet so reluctant to entrust their seeds to the earth. In entrusting them to the earth, they were still entrusting them to the sun. Thus a differentiation came about. Here, in the first two metamorphoses, we can only speak of the ancient precursors of the insect world. To entrust things to the cosmos, the outer planets and the sun still meant, at that time, entrusting them to the earth as well. Only as the earth grew dense, and acquired water and the magnetic forces of the Moon stage did conditions change and give rise to greater differentiation.

Now let us assume that all this belongs to the upper realm of warmth and air. And now let us take what belongs to the lower realm, that of water and earth. Let us consider the seeds that were destined to be entrusted to the earth while others were held back and not entrusted to the earth but instead only to the solar realm within earthly conditions.

So we have the seeds entrusted to the earth during the third period of metamorphosis, that of Moon. These seeds fall under the sway of the earth, of the watery action of the Moon earth, in contrast to the insect seeds or eggs that were only under the sway of the sun and the outer planetary system. By falling under the sway of earthly and watery influences, they became plant seeds, while the seeds that stayed in the upper realm remained germinal insects. And in this way, as the third stage of ancient earth metamorphosis began, germinal plants formed through this transformation of Sun evolution into the nature of Moon earth. So we can consider in this light the whole development we see unfolding under the influence of the cosmos from egg through caterpillar and pupa to butterfly. As the plant seed becomes earthly, the butterfly does not accompany this development, but instead the seed entrusted to earth—and now no longer to the sun— gives rise to the plant root as the first thing to emerge from the seed. And instead of a caterpillar that crawls into the sphere of forces emanating from Mars, a leaf develops and as it were crawls upwards in spiral forms. The leaf is therefore the caterpillar that has fallen under the sway of earthly forces. Take a look at the crawling caterpillar: it is the upper correspondence to the lower realm's metamorphosis of plant leaf from root, and in turn from the seed that was transposed from the solar realm into that of earth.

If we trace this development further as the plant grows, then, ever more contracted towards the calyx, we find a correspondence with the pupa. And finally, coming full circle, the blossom opens as equally colourful counterpart to the airborne butterfly. In the same way that the butterfly lays its egg, the seed of future life develops again in the blossom. So looking up into the air we can see the butterfly as plant raised into the air. The butterfly, developing from egg to winged creature under the sun's influence and that of the outer planets, is the same as the plant below under the earth's influence. In the case of the plant, this occurs in a cycle of influence passing from the earth to the moon, then to Venus and Mercury, returning again to the earth's influence. The seed returns to the influence of the earth.

The following two thoughts therefore express a great secret of nature:

Look upon the plant:
It is the butterfly
Bound to the earth.

Look upon the butterfly:
It is the plant
Freed by the cosmos.

The plant—the butterfly bound by the earth! The butterfly—the plant liberated from the earth by the cosmos!

If we consider the butterfly, or in fact any insect, from its germinal form through to the fluttering, winged creature, we find that it is the plant raised into the air and configured by the cosmos as airborne form. If we consider the plant we find it is the butterfly constrained below. The butterfly egg becomes the seed under the sway of the earth; the caterpillar metamorphoses into leaf forms; the pupa metamorphoses into upward contractions towards the calyx. Then the plant develops as blossom, finally, what unfolds in the butterfly. No wonder then that such an intimate relationship exists between the world of butterflies and insects in general, and the plant realm. The spiritual beings underlying the life of insects and butterflies have to say something like this: There below are our relatives, we must keep close to them and connect with them. We must connect with them, enjoying their saps and nectars, for they are our brothers. They are brothers that migrated down into the realm of earth and became bound below, entering into a different existence.

And in turn, the spirits that ensoul plants could look up to the butterflies and see there the heavenly relatives of earthly plants.

So we cannot understand the world through abstractions, which are unable to give us real insight. The greatest artistry works and weaves in the cosmos. The cosmos configures everything in accordance with laws which are profoundly satisfying to the artistic sense. We cannot understand the butterfly that has sunk down into the realm of earth without transforming abstract thoughts as an artist does. No one can understand how the butterfly is a flower blossom lifted into the air by light and cosmic forces without, once again, bringing artistic life and movement into abstract ideas. Really perceiving the deep inner connection between nature's plants and creatures is something enormously uplifting and enlightening.

It is a remarkable thing to see an insect sitting on a plant and at the same time to see how the astral realm holds sway over the flower blossom. The plant strives away from the earthly domain. The plant's yearning for the heavens over-arches the shimmering petals of its flower. The plant itself cannot satisfy this yearning. But the butterfly and all it embodies shines down towards it from the cosmos; and the plant sees in it the fulfilment of its wishes. Thus we have a wonderful mutuality within earthly conditions, whereby the plant world's longings are fulfilled by the presence of the insects, and by the world of butterflies in particular. What the colourful flower yearns for as it shines out into cosmic space is, one can say, recognized and fulfilled by the brightly shimmering butterfly that approaches it. Longing that emanates warmth meets fulfilment shining in from the heavens, in reciprocity and mutual encounter between the world of flowers and the world of butterflies. We should open our eyes to this mutuality.

Having described this connecting bridge with the world of plants, I will be able to enlarge on our observations in the next few days. We can now include the plant world in the living context of human and animal kingdoms and can thus gradually elaborate the relationship of human beings to the whole earth. But first it was necessary to connect the fluttering air-plant, the butterfly, to the earthbound butterfly, the plant. The plant within the earth is the rooted butterfly, while the butterfly is the flying plant. Having understood this connection between the earthbound plant and heaven-freed butterfly, this bridge between the plant world and the animal world will enable us to pass untroubled beyond all trivial concepts such as abiogenesis.[15] Prosaic concepts of this kind do not come anywhere near the realms of the universe we need to penetrate. We only begin to penetrate them when we can lead prosaic concepts into artistic ones, forming ideas and pictures such as that of the heaven-derived butterfly egg entrusted only to the solar realm; or the plant developing only at a later stage, through metamorphosis of this butterfly egg, into a seed which is now no longer entrusted to solar conditions but instead to earthly ones.

6. The Butterfly's Spiritualization of Matter

Lecture given in Dornach on 27 October 1923

These lectures are concerned with interrelationships in the world and the cosmos, the inner connection between phenomena and creatures of all kinds. We have already seen many things that a merely external grasp of phenomena cannot penetrate. We found—and illustrated with a couple of examples—that every species has its part to play in the whole context of cosmic existence. Today, recapitulating a little, I would like to look at some species we have already discussed, and once again consider what has been said about the nature of butterflies over the last few days. I elaborated on the nature of butterflies in contrast to plants, and we saw that the butterfly is really a creature that belongs to the light—in so far as light is modified by the power of the outer planets, by Mars, Jupiter and Saturn. Thus if we want to understand the true nature of the butterfly, we have to look up into higher regions of the cosmos and see how these regions grace and gift the earth with the butterfly being.

In fact, though, this gift of grace to the earth goes much deeper. You remember that we said the butterfly does not engage directly in earthly existence but only indirectly in so far as the sun is active in the earthly realm with its warmth and luminous power. The butterfly even lays its eggs in a place where they can remain under the sway of solar effects, and therefore they are not entrusted to the earth but really only to the sun. Then the caterpillar hatches out, and lives under the sway of Mars forces. The sun influence persists of course as well. The pupa is formed, and this is under Jupiter's influence. Then the butterfly emerges from the pupa, reflecting in its shimmering colours the luminous nature of the sun, united with the power of Saturn, within the earthly environment.

So really we see before us here within the earthly realm the direct activity of Saturn influence expressed in the manifold colours of butterfly life. But now let us recall that the substances we meet in the universe are of two kinds: the purely material substances of the earth and then also spiritual substances. On another occasion I pointed out the remarkable fact that our own metabolic-limb system is based upon spiritual substance whereas our head relies upon physical substance. In the lower realm of the human organism, spiritual substance is permeated by physical forces, by gravity and the other earthly forces. Earthly substance that is conveyed upwards to the human head through the whole metabolism, circulation, nerve activity, and so forth, is permeated there by supersensible, spiritual forces that are reflected in our thinking, our picturing capacity. Thus we have spiritualized physical matter in our head whereas in the metabolic-limb system we have spiritual substantiality that has been rendered earthly.

This spiritualized matter is in fact something we find above all in the butterfly. By remaining in the solar realm it only appropriates earthly matter—speaking metaphorically of course—as though in the form of the finest dust. The butterfly takes possession of earthly matter only as the finest dust. It also procures its food from sun-permeated earthly substances. It unites its being only with what is sun-permeated. One can say that the butterfly takes the very finest of all earthly substance and raises it to the fullest spiritualization. If you look at a butterfly wing you really have before you the most spiritualized earthly matter. It is the most spiritualized earthly material by virtue of the colours that permeate and penetrate it entirely.

The butterfly is in fact a creature that lives entirely in spiritualized earthly matter. With eyes of spirit one can even see how in a certain sense the butterfly disdains the body it has in the midst of its wings since its whole attention, its whole group soul nature, really resides in a glad enjoyment of its coloured wings.

Just as one can observe a butterfly and admire its shimmering colours, so one can admire its fluttering joy at these colours. Actually we should already cultivate this in children, this pleasure in the spirituality that flutters about in the air and which is really fluttering joy, joy at the delicate play of colours. In this regard butterfly nature is very wonderfully nuanced. But all this is in turn founded on something else.

In considering the bird, represented by the eagle, we saw that it can bear spiritualized earthly substance into the world of spirit when it dies; and that its task in cosmic terms is to spiritualize earthly matter and thus, as a bird, do what humans cannot. In our head we also spiritualize earthly matter to a certain extent, but we cannot take this earthly matter with us into the world we experience between death and a new birth. If we were to do so, if we were to bear this spiritualized earthly matter of our head into the world of spirit, we would have to continually endure an unspeakable, unbearable, shattering pain.

The world of birds, represented by the eagle, is capable of doing this, thus in fact creating a connection between what is earthly and what is not. Earthly matter is as it were first slowly led over into spirit, and the race of birds has the task of passing this spiritualized earthly substance to the universe.

When the earth eventually reaches the end and goal of its existence, we will be able to say that its substance, its matter, has been spiritualized, and that birds were present within earthly existence, within its whole balanced interplay of forces, in order to bear spiritualized earthly matter back into spirit land.

Things are somewhat different with butterflies. The butterfly spiritualizes earthly matter still more than the bird. The bird comes much closer to the earth than the butterfly does, as I will describe below. But by virtue of the fact that it never leaves the solar region, the butterfly is able to spiritualize its substance to such an extent that it can continually pass spiritualized matter to its earthly surroundings, to its cosmic earthly surroundings while it lives, and not just at its death as the bird does.

Picture for a moment what a grandiose thing this is within the whole interplay of cosmic forces: the earth where the world of butterflies flutters in the most manifold ways, continually streaming spiritualized earthly matter out into cosmic space, giving it up to the cosmos! This insight can kindle quite different feelings in us about the butterfly world, this girdle of butterflies around the earth.

We can gaze into this fluttering world and realize that these fluttering creatures ray out something even better than sunlight: they shine spirit light out into the cosmos. Our modern materialistic science pays little attention to anything spiritual; and therefore it really has no means of grasping such things, which belong to the whole balance and interplay of forces in the world. But they really are present, just as physical effects are, and are more vital than physical effects. What streams out from the butterflies into spirit land will work on long after the earth has disintegrated. The matter which physicists and chemists study today will come to an end with the end of earthly existence. If there was an observer sitting out in the cosmos, and had long enough to watch, he would see how spirit-matter, matter that has become spirit, is continually shining out into spirit land; how the earth shines and streams out its own being into cosmic space and how all birds after their death shine out into the cosmos what appears like a spray of sparks, continually kindling sparks. Along with the sprinkling effervescence from the spirit light of birds, a shimmering gleam also rays out from butterflies.

If we turn our attention to that other gleaming world, the starry firmament, such insights can lead us beyond believing that the light shining down from them is composed only of what spectroscopes can measure—or rather what the spectroscopist fantasizes and projects into his readings. What shines down to earth from the stars is, equally, the outcome of living beings in other worlds, just as what shines out from the earth into the cosmos comes from living beings. As a modern physicist one looks at a star and pictures something like a lit, inorganic flame—something like that. Naturally this is utter nonsense, for what we see up there is the outcome, the emanation, of life, soul and spirit.

Let us now pass inward once more, if I may put it like this, from the butterfly girdle encircling the earth to the birds. If we now picture what we know, we find there are three adjoining regions. In descending order they are: light ether, warmth ether and air. Above these are other regions, and below them also other regions. We have the light ether, the warmth ether—which in fact can be divided into two layers, the one an earthly warmth layer, the other a cosmic warmth layer, two types of warmth, not one, the first of which is really earthly, telluric in origin, and the other which is derived from the cosmos. Both are in constant interplay with each other. Then, adjoining the warmth ether, we have the air. After this come water and earth; and above we have chemical ether and then life ether.

The butterflies primarily belong to the light ether, and the light ether itself is the medium in which luminosity draws the caterpillar forth from the butterfly egg; luminosity is really what induces it to hatch, primarily. Things are different in the case of the birds. They lay their eggs, and these require brood warmth, while the butterfly's egg is simply entrusted to sun and solar forces. The bird egg, by contrast, enters the region of more earthly warmth. The bird exists in the warmth ether region, and really overcomes what is merely air.

Although the butterfly also flies in the air it is really entirely a creature of light. Light permeates the air, but the butterfly chooses light existence rather than air existence in this light-air realm. Air only bears it. Air offers the waves and currents upon which, you can say, it floats about, but its real element is light. The bird flies in the air but its real element is warmth, the varying eddies of warmth in the air; and in a certain sense it overcomes the air. The bird is after all also inwardly an air being. The bones of mammals and human bones are filled with bone marrow, while bird bones are hollow and only filled with air. As far as our bones are concerned we are marrow beings, while the bird really consists of air: its marrow is pure air. If you look at a bird's lungs you will find a large number of sacs, air sacs around the lungs. When a bird breathes, the air not only enters its lungs but also these air sacs, and from there the air passes into the hollow bones. If we took all flesh and feathers away from a bird, if we could remove its bones, we would be left with a creature consisting of nothing but air, shaped by the inner extent of its lungs and the inner air content in the bones. If you picture this form of the bird, it would still be entirely bird-shaped. Inside the flesh-and-bone eagle there is also an air eagle. When the bird breathes, its respiration engenders warmth. This warmth is conveyed to its inner air which infuses all its limbs, giving rise to a warmth differential compared with the outer environment: inner warmth and outer warmth. The bird really lives in this difference of warmth levels between the air's outer warmth and that within the bird's own air organism—it lives in a warmth differential, a difference of warmth levels. And if you were to ask a bird how it finds its body, it would tell you—if you understood bird language—that it experiences the bones and the flesh and feathers it carries somewhat as you would feel with suitcases tied all over you, to left and right, and on your back and head. You would not say that the suitcases tied on all over you are your body, but that you are carrying them; and likewise the bird regards itself only as the warmed air within it, and sees everything else just as luggage it has to carry around in earthly existence. Its luggage is the bones that really only encapsulate the bird's real air body. Basically we have to see that the bird lives entirely in the element of warmth and the butterfly in the element of light. All physical substance, before the butterfly spiritualizes it, is really even weightier for it than luggage. It is still more remote from the butterfly. We could call it something like furniture.

As we ascend into these regions and to the creatures there, we come to something that we really should not judge by physical standards. When we judge such things according to physical criteria this is rather like trying to draw a person with hair growing out of a suitcase he's carrying on his head, drawing him with luggage growing out of his arms and a rucksack growing from his back like some kind of excrescence or deformity. If we were to draw a human figure like this, it would correspond to the idea which a materialist has of the bird. This is not the bird but rather the luggage it carries. The bird really feels as if it carries quite a burden in the form of this luggage. It would prefer to be free as the wind, not burdened, would like to wander freely through the world as a warm air creature. The rest of its being is the freight it carries. And it pays its tribute to cosmic existence by spiritualizing this burden and sending it out into spirit land when it dies, while the butterfly does this already during its lifetime.

The bird breathes and employs the air as I described, but the butterfly is different. Butterflies do not breathe by anything like the same means as the so-called higher animals (in fact they are not 'higher' but just larger in size). The butterfly really only breathes through tubes that pass inwards from its outer surface and which swell somewhat so that it can store air as it flies, remaining undisturbed by any need to breathe. It only breathes through tubes that enter its interior. This enables it to absorb the light, contained in the air it breathes in, into its whole body. This again is something very different.

Picturing this schematically you can imagine a higher animal with lungs: oxygen enters the lungs and connects with the blood via the heart. Blood has to flow into the heart and lungs in order to come into contact with oxygen in these larger animals, and also in human beings. Things look quite different in the butterfly. Here is the butterfly [*drawing*] and the tubules enter it everywhere, branching and dividing. Oxygen flows in everywhere and likewise divides and spreads so that air penetrates the body everywhere.

In us and in the so-called higher animals, the air as such only enters as far as the lungs. In the butterfly the external air, along with its light content, spreads throughout the butterfly's whole body. The bird diffuses the air into its hollow bones while the butterfly shows it is a creature of light both in an inner and outer sense by diffusing the airborne light throughout its body, thus becoming light-filled within. The bird is really inwardly warmed air, while the butterfly is really entirely composed of light. Its body also consists of light, while warmth is really a burden for it, a kind of weighty luggage. It flutters in nothing but the light, and really builds its body out of light. When we see butterflies fluttering in the air we ought really to see them as nothing other than light beings: beings of light joyous in their colours and the play of colours. All the rest is garment and luggage. Outward appearance deceives us and we need to go beyond it to see what the creatures in our natural environment are really made of.

There are those who have learned certain superficial things, for instance from oriental wisdom, and say that the world is 'maya' or illusion. But saying this really tells us nothing. We have to study details to see in what way things are maya. We understand something of maya when we realize that the bird's true being is not as it appears externally, but that really it is a warm being of air. The butterfly is not as it seems, but is really a fluttering being of light. It is composed mostly of joy in the play of colours that arises in its wings when the fine dust of earthly matter is permeated with colour, thus attaining the first level of spiritualization and spreading out into the spiritual universe, the spiritual cosmos.

Here we have, in a way, two levels: the butterfly dwelling in the light ether in our earthly environment; and the bird inhabiting the warmth ether there. Now we come to a third level. When we descend further into the air element, we find creatures that could not have existed at all at a certain period of our earth's evolution—for instance when the moon was still part of the earth and had not yet separated from it. While these creatures are also creatures of the air, live in the air, they are already very much under the sway of Earth evolution, of what is particular to the earth, that is, its gravity. Gravity has no purchase on the butterfly. It flutters joyfully in the light ether, feeling itself to be a creature born out of the light ether. The bird overcomes gravity by warming the air within it, making it warm air, which is borne up and carried by cold air. Thus birds also overcome gravity.

The creatures that have evolved to live in air but nevertheless cannot overcome gravity, having marrow-filled bones not hollow ones, and having no air sacs like the birds do, are the bats.

Bats are a very remarkable species. They do not overcome earth's gravity through the inner constitution of their bodies. They are not weightless as light, as butterflies are, nor light as warmth like the birds, but are subject to gravity and feel their flesh and bones to be part of them. This is why bats do not care for the element which composes the butterfly and in which it lives entirely, the element of light. They love twilight instead. They have to make use of the air, but they like it best when it does not bear light within it. They give themselves over to twilight and are really twilight creatures. Bats can only sustain themselves in the air with their bat wings which, one has to say, look somewhat like a caricature of wings. They are not real wings but instead skins stretched out between lengthened fingers, parachutes. By this means they keep themselves airborne. They only negotiate gravity by opposing it with something that is connected with it, as counterweight. But in consequence they are fully harnessed to the realm of earthly forces. Physical and mechanical construction can never, as such, reproduce butterfly flight, nor indeed the flight of birds—this will never fully succeed. Something else is always needed, other means of construction. But the flight of the bat can certainly be reproduced by means of earthly dynamics and mechanics.

The bat does not love the light, the light-permeated air, but at most the twilight air with a little light still playing through it. Another difference is this: when the bird looks, it is really always looking at what the air contains. Even the vulture looking down on a lamb feels it to be at the end of the airy sphere, as if just painted on the earth. Its sight is not mere seeing, either, but craving—as you will see if you really study the flight of a vulture that is pinpointing a lamb: its sight has a pronounced dynamic of will, of will and craving.

The butterfly sees what is on the earth as though in a mirror. For the butterfly the earth is a mirror. It sees what is in the cosmos. If you see a fluttering butterfly you have to picture it like this: it has no real interest in the earth itself, which reflects back to it what the cosmos contains like a mirror. The bird does not see earthly things but all that is in the air. The bat, finally, does begin to perceive what it flies through or what it flies past; and since it does not love the light, everything it sees is unpleasant to it. One can really say that the butterfly and the bird see in a very spiritual way. The bat is the first creature, in a descent from the upper realms downwards, that has to see in an earthly way, and does not enjoy this seeing. It does not like to see and therefore it has what one might call an embodied anxiety for everything it sees but does not wish to. It would like to whisk past things: it has to see but would rather not, and so wishes to dodge out of the way of everything. It is because it wants to dodge out the way of things that it listens with such wonderful acuity. The bat is in fact a creature that continuously listens to its own flight to discover if this flight might be impeded.

If you look at a bat's ears you can see they are tuned to world anxiety. They are very remarkable structures, which are really tuned to slipping secretively through the world, tuned to world anxiety. We can really only understand all this if we consider the bat in the context we have now placed it in.

Then there is another thing. The butterfly continually gives up spiritualized matter to the cosmos, and is the darling of Saturn influences. Now you will remember that I spoke of Saturn as the great bearer of our planetary system's memory. The butterfly is intimately connected with our planet's capacity for memory. In the butterfly live memorizing thoughts. The bird—as I said previously—is really entirely head; and as it flies through the warmed air it is really a living, flying thought in cosmic space. The capacity for thoughts that we have, which is also connected with the warmth ether, is bird nature, eagle nature within us. The bird is flying thought. The bat, however, is flying dream, the flying dream image of the cosmos.

Thus the earth is surrounded by a weft of butterflies, which are cosmic memory, while the race of birds is cosmic thinking and the bat is cosmic dream, cosmic dreaming. The bats swishing through the twilight are actually the flying dreams of the cosmos. Just as a dream loves the twilight, so the cosmos shows its love for the twilight by sending bats flitting through it. You can see the lasting thoughts of memory embodied in the earth's girdle of butterflies, thoughts living in the present moment in the girdle of birds around the earth, and dreams embodied as bats flying about in the earth's environs. When we enter fully into the form of bats we can feel how closely they are related to dreaming! There is no other way to consider this creature than by thinking: 'You're dreaming, this is something that shouldn't be there, that is as much at odds with all other natural creatures as the dream is at odds with ordinary physical reality.'

We saw that the butterfly sends spiritualized substance into spirit land during its lifetime, while the bird does this at death. What about the bat? During its life the bat gives off spiritualized substance, especially as this lives in the stretched skins of its 'wings', between its separate finger-bones. It does not, however, give this spiritualized substance up to the cosmos but instead emits it into the earth's atmosphere. In consequence, what one can call spirit pearls are continually created in the air. And thus the earth is surrounded by the continual outstreaming glimmer of spirit matter from butterflies, by the scattering spray of what comes from dying birds; but then also, radiating back to the earth, these strange inclusions in the air where bats emit what they spiritualize. These are the spiritual forms one always sees when one watches the flight of a bat. It will always have something like a comet trailing behind it. It emits spirit matter, but does not send this out into the cosmos but pushes it back into the physical matter of earth, pushes it back into the air. Just as we see the physical bat flitting about with our physical eyes, so we can also see the corresponding spiritual forms of the bats flitting through the air, swishing through the air. And while the air is of course composed of oxygen, nitrogen and other constituents, we also have to realize that it includes the spiritual influence of the bats.

However strange and paradoxical this sounds, the dream

race of bats emits tiny ghosts into the air which then combine into a common mass. In geology, the name magma is given to a stratum of still soft stony mass under the earth's surface. Likewise we could speak of a spirit magma in the air which originates in the emissions of bats.

In olden times, when people still possessed an instinctive clairvoyance, they were often very sensitive to this spiritual magma—as some people today are still sensitive to more material secretions such as bad smells. One might regard this as a more vulgar version of ancient, instinctive clairvoyant sensitivity to what was present in the air as bat residues.

They took steps to protect themselves against this. And in some mystery schools there were very specific formulations for shielding yourself against these bat residues, to prevent them gaining power over you. After all, we do not just breathe in oxygen and nitrogen with the air, but also these bat residues. Today people do not consider shielding themselves against these bat residues: they may often be highly sensitive to smells but have no sense of bat residues in the air. Thus they swallow them down without any feeling of distaste. It is really quite remarkable: people who are otherwise very squeamish just gulp down what I am speaking of without a thought. But it goes into them—not into the physical or etheric body, but into the astral body.

All this may seem somewhat strange, and is indeed remarkable. Initiation science does actually lead us into the inner context of phenomena. In fact these bat residues are the choicest food for what I have described to you in these lectures as 'the dragon'.[16] But first human beings have to breathe them in. And the dragon can best get a purchase on human nature and reside within it if we allow our instincts to be permeated by these bat residues. Then they whirl about in us, and the dragon devours them, growing fat—naturally in a spiritual sense—on this food, and gains power over the human being in all sorts of ways. So today we need to protect ourselves against this once again. Protection can come from what has been described here as the new form of Michael's battle with the dragon.[17] The inner empowerment we gain when we take up the Michael impulse shields us against the nourishment the dragon seeks, and thus we protect ourselves against the bat residue in the atmosphere, which should not by rights be there.

There is no need to be reticent about drawing truths from the inner context of reality if we really wish to penetrate the world's inner aspects. The generally acknowledged way in which people search for truth nowadays does not lead to anything real but instead, mostly, only to something dreamlike, to maya. Truth has to be sought in the realm where we find all physical existence interwoven with spiritual existence. Here we can only approach reality if we consider it as we have done here.

Creatures present in any realm are there for good purposes or bad ones. In the universal context every phenomenon or entity is connected with every other. In the view of materialists, butterflies flutter, birds fly and bats flit—and that's all there is to it. But this view is like a somewhat inartistic person who hangs all sorts of clashing pictures up in a room which have no inner connection with each other. For the ordinary observer the creatures flying about in the world have no inner connection because he sees none. But in fact everything in the cosmos occupies a position that is connected with all the rest of the cosmos. Whether butterfly, bird or bat, everything in the world has its meaning and purpose.

Those who care to ridicule such things can of course do so.

People have mocked before. Famous academies have stated that meteoric rocks cannot exist because iron cannot fall from the sky, and so on. So people will very likely ridicule what I have said today about the functions of bats, but this should not prevent us imbuing modern civilization with knowledge of the spirit.

7. Butterfly Corona, Earth Evolution and Reincarnation

From a lecture in Dornach, 28 October 1923

[. . .] If we look at the human being in his current form and ask ourselves what the oldest part of him is in terms of evolution, we find this to be the human head. This human head developed its earliest form in the period when the earth was still at the Saturn stage of development and metamorphosis. The Saturn stage consisted, though, of warmth substance alone, and the human head at that time was really swelling, weaving waves of warmth, subsequently assuming an airy form during the Sun stage, and later acquiring fluid form— thus becoming a flowing, trickling entity—during the Moon stage. It only acquired its solid, bony encapsulation during the Earth stage of our planet's evolution. Thus an entity very hard for us to conceive nowadays by external means was present during the ancient Saturn period—an entity that was an ancient precursor of the human head. At the same time that the human head was developing in this way, the precursors of the butterflies were developing too. Later we will consider other insects, but let us stay with the butterflies for now. If we trace evolution from Old Saturn down to today, to earthly existence as we know it, we see that originally the precursor of the human head developed in the form of very rarefied substance and at the same time the precursors of today's fluttering butterflies were forming. Both evolutionary paths continued. The human being became increasingly internalized, coming to express soul qualities that originate within him—in other words, a being that rays outwards from within. The butterfly, by contrast, is a creature upon whose exterior surface, we can say, the cosmos unfolds all its loveliness from without. The butterfly is a being that has as it were received the passing imprint of all the beauty and majesty present in the cosmos, as I have described. Thus we have to picture the butterfly as a mirror image of the upper realms of the cosmos, whereas we human beings absorb and enclose the higher cosmos in ourselves. Thus it becomes an inner soul experience, a soul concentration of the cosmos which then emanates outwards and gives the human head its form. In the human head we have something formed from within outwards whereas the butterfly is formed from without inwards. Someone who observes these things as a seer learns things of huge significance when he seeks to fathom the most ancient secrets, the Saturn secrets of the human head, seeks to discover what forces have actually been at work within the brain and its encapsulation. In doing so he has to take his lead from what is apparent everywhere in the external world, and which rays in everywhere: he has to study the butterflies. To acquaint yourself with the real miracles of your head, study the miracles involved in the butterfly's development in nature. The seer observes the magnificence of the cosmos and discovers these connections.

As we trace evolution further from the Saturn to the Sun stage, a being develops with a further elaboration of the head, an airy reconfiguration or airy metamorphosis. This attaches itself as fine substance which then later develops into the forms of the chest, the human respiratory and heart structures. So initially—during the Saturn stage—we primarily have the metamorphic form that embodies the head, though this is not fully present until a later period. Then we come to Sun evolution and we find the human being formed of head and chest. But at the same time, during the latter phase of the Saturn period and the first phase of the Sun period, the aspect develops that is represented by or embodied in the eagle. In the initial phase of the Sun period the birds appear, while in the second phase of the Sun period appear the first signs of the animal species which are really chest animals—such as the lion, and also other chest animals. The precursors of such animals are found during Sun evolution. [. . .]

As we pass on into the Moon period of earth's evolution, which introduces the fluid element [. . .] the precursors of the digestive system develop. On Old Sun, in conditions that are composed of light-permeated, light-illumined air, the evolving human being needs only a respiratory system to nourish him, one that is closed off below. Here the human being is just head and respiratory organ. Then, on Old Moon, the digestive system attaches itself so that the human being comes to be formed of head, chest and abdomen. And since everything on Old Moon is composed of watery substance, during this period the human being has outgrowths that bear him swimming through the water. Arms and legs really only develop during the Earth phase of planetary evolution, once gravity takes hold and elaborates the gravity-oriented limbs. During the Moon period, the digestive organs develop but still in a quite different form from their later appearance. This digestive system does not yet need to absorb all that serves free, voluntary movements of the limbs. [. . .]

Once again certain creatures are associated with this evolution. To the butterflies, birds and species represented by the lion are now also added those focused primarily on digestion. During Old Moon, we have, for example, what the cow embodies. [. . .] The cow develops during the first phase of Moon evolution, but then come other creatures that acquire their initial predisposition during the last phase of Moon evolution. [...] These creatures remain at the stage that the human being bears in his stomach. Just as the eagle and butterfly are associated with the human head, the lion with the chest and the cow with the abdomen [...] so amphibians and reptiles—thus toads, frogs, snakes, lizards and so forth—are, if I can put it like this, associated with the human abdomen, the human digestive tract. During the second phase of Moon evolution they arise in a coarse form and are really wandering stomachs and guts, wandering stomachs and intestines.

[...] Look at the butterflies and the birds and you will see their earthly forms. But from previous accounts you know that the butterfly is really a being of light that has as it were acquired earthly substance in passing. If the butterfly itself could tell you what it is, it would tell you that it has a body of light and that it bears the earthly matter that has attached itself to it like external luggage. Likewise the bird is a creature of the warm air, for the bird's true nature is actually the warm air diffused through it while the rest of it is the luggage it bears around with it. These creatures, which today preserve their nature of light or warmth but only in earthly raiment, fluid raiment, were the ones that evolved earliest in the whole of Earth evolution. These creatures also have forms which will remind anyone who can perceive the period we pass in the world of spirit before descending into earthly life, of what we experience there. Certainly their forms are earthly, for earthly substance has attached itself to them. But if you rightly picture those floating, weaving luminous beings the butterflies and think away what has attached itself to them as earthly substance, and do this also for the bird, picturing instead the energy mass that makes the bird into a warm being of air, and its plumage only shining rays, then these beings—which only appear as they do through their outer raiment, and only have the size they do because of this outer garb—will remind us of beings we know before we descend to the earth, reminding us also of this descent.

If you gaze into the world of spirit in this way you can see that the butterflies and the birds show us something that reminds us of the spirit forms we lived amongst before we descended to earth, the beings of the higher hierarchies. If we look at butterflies and birds with real understanding, we find they are a small, metamorphosed memory of the forms we had around us as spirit forms before we descended into earthly evolution. Because earthly matter is so heavy and has to be overcome, the butterflies contract what is really their gigantic form into a miniature scale. If you could separate out from a butterfly all that is earthly matter it would be able to expand into the form of an archangel, a spirit being, a luminous being. The creatures that inhabit the air are in fact earthly reflections of what lives in higher regions in spiritual form. In the time of ancient, instinctive clairvoyance, therefore, it was self-evident for people to create artistic, symbolic images of the spirit beings of the higher hierarchies based on the forms of flying animals. This has its inner justification. Fundamentally, the physical forms of butterflies and birds are the physical metamorphoses of spirit beings. The spirit beings themselves did not metamorphose into these creatures, but they are nevertheless metamorphosed images of them, though naturally different entities.

Returning to something I said previously therefore, you will also understand the following. I said that the butterfly, which is really a being of light, continually sends spirit-permeated matter out into the cosmos during its lifetime.

Borrowing a term from solar physics, I would like to call this spirit-permeated earthly matter sent out into the cosmos the 'butterfly corona'. The butterfly corona continually rays out into the cosmos. But into this butterfly corona there also streams what the birds give up to the cosmos when they die. Thus the spiritualized matter of birds shines in, too, to what rays out into the cosmos. Seen spiritually from without, therefore, we have the sight of a gleaming corona emanating from the butterflies—maintained in winter in accordance with certain laws—and at the same time, integrated with this but in a more raylike form, we see what flows out from the birds.

You see, when we set about descending from the world of spirit into the physical world, what first calls us into earthly existence is this singular emanation of spiritualized earthly matter. And the rays of the bird corona are felt more as forces that draw us inwards. So here we have a still deeper meaning of what lives in the atmosphere. In all that lives and weaves in reality we have to seek the spiritual aspect, and only then do we begin to grasp the significance of different realms of existence. The earth as it were entices the human being to reincarnate by sending out the luminous emanations of the butterfly corona and the bird corona into the cosmos. These are things that, after we have spent a certain period in the purely spiritual world between death and a new birth, call us back again into a new life on earth. It is no wonder, therefore, if it is hard for us to grasp and explain the complex feelings we rightly have when we look upon the world of butterflies and birds, for the underlying reality of this realm lies deep in our subconscious. What we really have there is a memory of our longing for a new life on earth.

And this in turn is connected with what I have often said

about what happens to us after we pass through the portal of death: our head is really dispersed and the rest of our organism—in terms of forces of course, not matter—is reconfigured into the head of our next life on earth. As we strive downwards towards incarnation, therefore, we are really striving towards the head; and the head is the first thing to develop in the human embryo in a form that resembles what it will later be in the human form. All this, the development towards the form of the head, is intimately related with what works and weaves in the world of flying creatures, which really draws us down from supersensible into sensory life.

Then, having acquired our head organization during embryonic development, the digestive organism and so forth forms in the mother's womb. Just as what is above, the head, is connected with the nature of warmth and air, with warmth and light, the element of earthly moisture is connected with what we acquired later in the course of evolution and which is now membered into us during embryonic development. This earthly, watery element must however be prepared for us in a very special way, that is, in the mother's womb. Where it only forms outside in the telluric realm, spread out through the earthly domain, it gives rise to the lower animal forms, the amphibians and reptiles, and then later also fish and still lower animals. [...] With the same forces we use for digestion, the outer cosmos forms snakes, frogs, toads and lizards. Anyone who wishes to study the human intestine—forgive me but actually nothing in nature is ugly, and all needs to be seen objectively—to discover its inner nature and its powers of excretion should study the frogs and toads, for there attaches outwardly to the toad what works from within outwards in the human large intestine. This is perhaps not so beautiful to contemplate as what I described in the case of the butterfly, but in nature everything must be considered with equal interest and objectivity. [...]

We can study the whole human being, from head down to limbs by studying what surrounds us in nature. World and human being belong together. And we can say [...] that where our senses engage with the world, there is mutual interaction between what emerges from within outwards in the human being and what has passed inwards from without in the cosmos. In this sense the human being is a small world, a microcosm in relation to the macrocosm. We contain within us all the wonders and mysteries of this macrocosm, but in reversed evolutionary direction. [...]

Appendix: Planetary Evolution

From a lecture in Dornach on 26 October 1923[18]

As I have described in my book *Occult Science*, the earth's evolution within the cosmos takes its point of departure from a metamorphosis of very ancient Saturn conditions. We should picture this Saturn state and its metamorphosis as containing everything that belongs to our planetary system. The various planets in our solar system, from Saturn down to our moon, were at that ancient time still contained within Old Saturn—which, as you know, consisted solely of warmth ether—in a dissolved form. Thus Saturn, which had not yet acquired the density of air but was still warmth ether as I said, contained an etheric solution of all that was subsequently to become separately configured and individualized in the various planets.

As the second stage of metamorphosis in earth's evolution, we can then distinguish what I have referred to generally as the ancient Sun stage. Here the fire body of Saturn gradually transformed into the airy body, the light-permeated, light-illumined and radiant airy body of the planetary condition of Sun.

In a third stage of metamorphosis, after former conditions had first been repeated, distinguishing Sun nature, which at that point still encompassed the earth and the moon, from Saturn as separate from it, we reach the Moon stage of planetary evolution—you can read all about this in detail in *Occult Science*. Here the sun and what constitutes a unity of earth and moon separate from each other. I have often described how the kingdoms of nature we know today were not yet present at that stage. Earth was not present as a mineral mass but—if I can put it like this—had a hornlike substantiality such that the solid constituents emerged like horn; horn-type rocks emerged as it were from what had become the watery Moon mass. Then, in the fourth metamorphosis, our present earthly conditions evolved. [...]

We have to be clear that whatever once existed returns again and continues to exist in later evolutionary stages. What existed as an ancient fire sphere, as Saturn, remains as warmth substance in all subsequent metamorphoses. [...] Wherever we encounter air or gaseous bodies, this is the residue of Sun evolution. When we gaze out into sun-irradiated air, then we should sense and recognize the qualities of that stage of evolution and grasp the fact that if it had never taken place our atmosphere would not have the relationship it does with sun rays, as an atmosphere into which sunlight falls from without. A later evolutionary stage, our present Earth metamorphosis, with the body of the earth surrounded by an atmosphere of air, can only exist by virtue of the fact that the sun once formed a unity with the earth, that the light of the sun itself shone within the earth, which as yet was only gaseous in nature; and therefore the earth at that time was a sphere of air which radiated inner light into the cosmos. [...] The sun rays have a deep inner relationship with the atmosphere, and this is an after-effect of the original unity of sun and earth. [...]

So that today, when we consider conditions on earth, we can recognize what remains of Saturn and Sun nature. We can say that all that exists as warmth and illumined air is Saturn-Sun. And when we look up we can discover that our atmosphere is imbued with Saturn and Sun influence which gradually evolved into our atmosphere as an after-effect of

Sun conditions. [...] If we look down, by contrast, we have instead the effects of the last two stages of earth's metamorphosis: we have the solid, firm aspect, the influence of weight leading into solidity; and we have all that is fluid, deriving from Moon earth. These two aspects of earth existence can be clearly distinguished from each other at the point where Sun conditions metamorphose into Moon conditions [...] between airy Saturn-Sun and watery Moon-Earth.

Sources

GA numbers refer to the complete edition of Rudolf Steiner's works.

1. Woven Sunlight: 19 October 1923, GA 230. See *Harmony of the Creative Word*, Rudolf Steiner Press 2001.
2. Metamorphoses: 8 October 1923, GA 351
3. Born out of Light: 15 October 1923, GA 302a. See *Balance in Teaching*, SteinerBooks 2007.
4. The Butterfly as an Image of the Immortal Soul: 11 August 1919, GA 296. See *Education as a Force for Social Change*, SteinerBooks 2007.
5. Butterfly Beings and Plant Nature: 26 October 1923, GA 230, part II. See *Harmony of the Creative Word*, Rudolf Steiner Press 2001.
6. The Butterfly's Spiritualization of Matter: 27 October 1923, GA 230 part II. See *Harmony of the Creative Word*, Rudolf Steiner Press 2001.
7. Butterfly Corona, Earth Evolution and Reincarnation: 28 October 1923, GA 230 part II. See *Harmony of the Creative Word*, Rudolf Steiner Press 2001.

Appendix: Planetary Evolution: 26 October 1923, GA 230, part II.

Notes

1. Maria Sibylla Merian (1647–1717) was a German scientist and artist. Her works contain detailed coloured plates, primarily of insects.
2. Jean-Henri Fabre (1823–1915), French entomologist and prolific author, known for his studies on insect behaviour. His *magnum opus*, the ten-volume *Souvenirs entomologiques*, was published between 1879 and 1907. Some of Fabre's most famous studies have been translated into English (see, for example, *The Insect World of J. Henri Fabre*, trans Alexander Teixeira de Mattos, Beacon Press, Boston, MA, 1991).
3. For more on the ethers as Steiner describes them, see: Ernst Marti, *The Four Ethers*, Schaumberg, 1984.
4. Letter from Andreas Suchantke, 1990.
5. Nelly Sachs (1891–1970), 'Abraham' in the cycle of poems 'Sternverdunkelung' from the collection *Fahrt ins Staublose*, Surkamp, Frankfurt/Main 1961.
6. Carrington Bonsor Williams, *British Immigrant Butterflies and Moths*, British Museum, 1936.
7. Cf. Andreas Suchantke, 'Biotoptracht und Mimikry bei afrikanischen Tagfaltern' in: Wolfgang Schad (ed), *Goetheanistische Naturwissenschaft*, vol. 3, Zoologie, Freies Geistesleben, Stuttgart 1985.
8. See R. Steiner, *Occult Science, an Outline*, for a full account of these stages of planetary evolution, which are also referred to in some passages in this book. See also the Appendix for a more extended passage on planetary evolution.
9. Cf. lectures of 9 and 10 September 1923, GA 228, pp. 85f., 89–94, 103–17 (German edition). See *Man in the Past, the Present and the Future*, Rudolf Steiner Press 1983.
10. Translator's note: The etheric body or life body, which we share with plants and animals, is connected with all life pro-

cesses and the circulation of fluids. The astral body, which we share with animals, is connected with all internalized soul life and emotion. Alone in all kingdoms of nature, humans also possess a self-aware ego or I as core spiritual entity that passes from earthly life to death and back again in many repeated and evolving incarnations.

11. See note 3 above.
12. See Appendix for passages from this lecture which go into greater detail on planetary evolution.
13. Translator's note: References to past and future planetary conditions of the earth should be distinguished from the planetary bodies of the same name that presently exist in the cosmos. In this book, former or present stages of evolution are distinguished by capitals, i.e. Sun, Moon or Earth stages.
14. In the lecture of 19 October 1923, GA 230, in this volume.
15. Translator's note: This is a hypothesis according to which life and biological processes are supposed to have arisen from inorganic matter.
16. See lectures in GA 223. *Michaelmas and the Soul Forces of Man*, SteinerBooks 1982.
17. Cf. for example *Michaelmas*, Rudolf Steiner Press, 2007.
18. Translator's note: These passages form part of the lecture of the same date that comes earlier in this volume (page 44).